WESLEY/LANGSHAW CORRESPONDENCE

CHARLES WESLEY, HIS SONS, AND THE LANCASTER ORGANISTS

EMORY TEXTS *AND* STUDIES
IN ECCLESIAL LIFE

General Editor: Channing R. Jeschke
Number 1: Wesley-Langshaw Correspondence

1993

WESLEY/LANGSHAW CORRESPONDENCE

CHARLES WESLEY, HIS SONS, AND THE LANCASTER ORGANISTS

Edited by Arthur W. Wainwright
In collaboration with Don E. Saliers

1993 SCHOLARS PRESS

EMORY TEXTS AND STUDIES IN ECCLESIAL LIFE

Wesley-Langshaw Correspondence

Edited by Arthur W. Wainwright
In collaboration with Don E. Saliers

© 1993
Emory University

Library of Congress Cataloging in Publication Data
Wesley-Langshaw correspondence: Charles Wesley, his sons, and the Lancaster organists/ edited by Arthur W. Wainwright in collaboration with Don E. Saliers.
    p. cm. — (Emory texts and studies in ecclesial life; 1)
    Includes index.
    ISBN 1-55540-848-6. — ISBN 1-55540-849-4 (pbk.)
    1. Wesley family—Correspondence. 2. Langshaw, John, 1718-1798—Correspondence. 3. Church musicians—England—Correspondence. 4. Church Music—Methodist Church—18th century. 5. Church music—England—18th century.   I. Wainwright, Arthur William. II. Saliers, Don E., 1937-
III. Series.
ML385.W35   1993
287'.092'2—dc20   93-25483
                                                                                    CIP

Published by Scholars Press
for
Emory University

*Publication of this book
was made possible by a gift
in honor of
Brittany Anne Hixon
and
Mary Elizabeth Hixon*

My dear Sir,

You have been wanting these days to Jacki Johnson. We shall be sorry to part with him —— What is not to You & his Mother. Most probably, who will see him again in August. Your other Son seems a very promising Gentleman. By & by he may bring his Brother & you into favor with Dr John who is Henry's Ward & probably reconciled. If he knew exactly how matters stand? Only Charles Wood not unnecessarily give them to Dr &c.

We have not yet heated You [?] altho' Decemb. —— which proved as good as you wish'd him.

I lately met with one of y[r] letters unanswered; but do not always complain

who wrote last. You are almost my only Correspondent. Indeed it is time for me to shake hands with all y[e] world at parting. Your night also cometh. Blessed is that Servant whom his Lord shall find watching. May this blessedness be yours & mine —— I am
with sincere affection
Your faithful Bro[r] & Servant
C Wesley

London
M June 8. 1779.

Letter No. 10.
Charles Wesley to John Langshaw.

Turnover

All my Brother's Societies know the King, because they all fear God. I wish the whole nation like them, or His. The Sons of his Mr. rejoice in the late Defeat of his Enemies. They curse our tyrants; but the brightest in their mouth.

We are so happy, & so is Yr in Jackie's prosperity. He writes a blessing to his Family, and a Credit to his Master. Wishing you truly happy in the love of Christ Jesus, I remain, my dear Sr

Your faithful loving serv.t
C. Wesley

Written in March 1784

Who can deny the Patriots their praise?
All Order is inverted in our days;
"King, Lords, & Commons" is not no more the thing
But Commons, Lords, & after that — The King:
We see the Subjects on their Sovereign's head
The Crown beneath the Mace, the RUMP above
   the Head!

Marÿbone

Letter No. 25.
Charles Wesley to John Langshaw.

CONTENTS

General Editor's Preface / xi

Preface / xiii

Abbreviations / xv

Introduction / 1

The Correspondence / 15

Index of Names / 89

GENERAL EDITOR'S PREFACE

Emory Texts and Studies in Ecclesial Life is a new series to be published by Emory University. The series will present unique material of significance to scholarship from the university libraries' resources in religion and theology. Since Emory's founding in 1836 by Georgia Methodists, print and manuscript collections of exceptional strength have been gathered in five areas: the Richard C. Kessler Reformation Collection, focused on early editions of the writings of Martin Luther, his friends, and his opponents; English religious life and thought from the Stuarts through the Victorian Era; European theological dissertations from the seventeenth through the nineteenth centuries; the Warrington-Pratt-Soule Collection of Hymnody and Psalmody; and material from sub-Saharan Africa that reflects contemporary religious life and thought in the region. Publications in this new series will include critical editions of manuscript texts, annotated bibliographies, and facsimile editions of important and rare imprints.

As the inaugural volume of this series, the Wesley-Langshaw Correspondence draws upon the university's extensive manuscript collection of unpublished letters from the Wesley family members and prominent early British Methodists. Two senior faculty members of Emory's Candler School of Theology, Arthur W. Wainwright, professor of New Testament and British Methodist minister, and Don E. Saliers, professor of theology and worship, join their skills and interests to share and illuminate this segment of early Methodist involvement in English musical life.

The series will continue with two volumes that draw upon the Richard C. Kessler Reformation Collection. Steven A. Crist, musicologist in Emory College, is preparing a facsimile edition of *Enchiridion Geistliker leder vnde Psalmen* (Magdeburg: Michael Lotther, 1536) with introduction and critical notes. The copy held at the Pitts Theology Library is the only known copy of this important early Lutheran hymnal in Low German, and it includes valuable manuscript notes and hymns written on the endpapers. For the second volume, Fred A. Grater, rare book bibliographer of the Pitts Theology Library, is preparing an annotated bibliography of the complete collection of over thirteen hundred titles. Art historians will also be interested in this volume, which will reproduce each title page.

From the collections of English religious life and thought, Peter C. Erb, professor of religion and culture at Wilfred Laurier University, is preparing a ground-breaking edition of the correspondence between Henry Edward Manning and William Ewart Gladstone. Two volumes will comprise their correspondence up to 1851, when Manning converted to Roman Catholicism, and a third volume will cover their later years.

We are grateful to Professors Wainwright and Saliers for their contributions in this initial offering and to the staff of the Special Collections Department of the Robert W. Woodruff Library for Advanced Studies at Emory for their assistance. Additional publications are planned, which will enhance the continuing value of this series for both church and scholarly communities.

Channing R. Jeschke, General Editor and
Margaret A. Pitts Professor of Theological Bibliography
Emory University
October 14, 1992

PREFACE

In 1989 the Special Collections Department of the Robert W. Woodruff Library of Emory University purchased a collection of thirty-two letters by Charles Wesley, his two sons, the musicians Charles Jr. and Samuel, and John Langshaw, organist of Lancaster Parish Church. This edition contains a transcription of the contents of this collection, together with an introduction and notes. In addition to the correspondence in Emory University's collection, the Methodist Collection, Drew University Library, contains a letter from Charles Wesley to John Langshaw (Letter 15, Sept. 25, 1780), and we are grateful for permission to include a transcription in this edition.

In the preparation of this edition Arthur Wainwright wrote the introduction and notes and was responsible for the transcription of the manuscript and for the research. Don Saliers collaborated in the project both in overall planning and negotiation and in consultation at each stage of the work's development.

Many people have been of assistance to us. Dr. Oliver A. Beckerlegge has shared his great knowledge of Wesley studies and his expertise in Wesley manuscripts, making many suggestions for improvements. Mr. Philip Olleson of Nottingham University provided important information about primary sources and drew attention to the letter that has been transcribed from the United Methodist Archives. Valuable assistance has also been given by Professor Frank Baker of Duke University, Professor Robert A. Smith of Emory University, Canon Maurice E. Bartlett, Vicar of Lancaster, Canon Malcolm Forrest, Rector of Wigan, and Dr. John A. Vickers.

The project was encouraged by the Charles Wesley Society and its current president, Dr. S. T. Kimbrough, Jr., by including our presentation of the

Wesley-Langshaw correspondence at its Second Annual Meeting, held at Princeton in October, 1991.

We are grateful to the staffs of libraries and research centers for their assistance, especially to Ms. Beverly D. Allen of the Robert W. Woodruff Library of Emory University and to Dr. M. Patrick Graham of the Pitts Theology Library of Emory University. Other institutions that have been very helpful in making their resources available are the Methodist Archives and Research Centre at the John Rylands University Library of Manchester, Drew University Library, the British Library, Lancaster Reference Library, the Library of the Royal Academy of Music, Marylebone Reference Library, and the Lancashire County Records Office in Preston.

This book would not have emerged without the initial support of Thomas Bertrand, the Secretary of Emory University, and his successor, Dr. Gary Hauk. The presence of the Wesley-Langshaw correspondence at Emory University and the conception of the series that this edition inaugurates are testimonies to the remarkable imagination and librarianship of Dr. Channing R. Jeschke, Librarian of the Pitts Theology Library. Finally, without a generous grant from Ms. Kathleen Ann Hall, the publication of this initial volume of the series would not have been possible. For her enthusiasm and support we are grateful.

A.W.W.
D.E.S.

ABBREVIATIONS

Alum. Cantab.	*Alumni Cantabrigienses: a Biographical List of All Known Students, Graduate and Holders of Office at the University of Cambridge from the Earliest Times to 1950.* Ed. J. Venn and J. A. Venn. 2 pts. in 10 vols. Cambridge: University Press, 1924-54.
Alum. Oxon.	*Alumni Oxonienses: the Members of the University of Oxford, 1715-1886.* Ed. Joseph Foster. 4 vols. in 2. Oxford: Parker & Co., 1887-88.
AV	Authorized Version (King James Version).
BCP	Book of Common Prayer. London, 1662.
BL	British Library.
Boeringer	Boeringer, James. *Organa Britannica: Organs in Great Britain, 1660-1860.* 3 vols. Lewisburg: Bucknell University Press; London and Toronto: Associated University Presses, 1983-89.
DNB	*Dictionary of National Biography.* 22 vols. London: Oxford University Press, 1921-22.
Grove^3	*A Dictionary of Music and Musicians.* 3rd. ed. Ed. H. C. Colles. 5 vols. New York: Macmillan, 1936.
MARC	Methodist Archives and Research Centre, John Rylands University Library of Manchester.

NG	*The New Grove Dictionary of Music and Musicians.* Ed. Stanley Sadie. 20 vols. London: Macmillan, 1980.
RAM, Wesley	Royal Academy of Music, MS. GB: Lam MS-L WESLEY, C. Wesley, Charles, "Notes on his sons' subscription concerts."
Shaw	Shaw, Watkins. *The Succession of Organists of the Chapel Royal and the Cathedrals of England and Wales from c.1538.* Oxford: Clarendon Press, 1991.
Thistlethwaite	Thistlethwaite, Nicholas. *The Making of the Victorian Organ.* Cambridge: Cambridge University Press, 1990.
Woodruff	John Wesley Collection, Special Collections Department, Robert W. Woodruff Library, Emory University.

INTRODUCTION

The Letters and their Writers

Between 1778 and 1827 Charles Wesley and his sons, Charles Jr. and Samuel, exchanged correspondence with John Langshaw and his son, both of whom were organists at the Priory and Parish Church of St. Mary, Lancaster. With the exception of one item, the letters were written at two different periods in the life of these families. Most of the correspondence comes from the first period, which was between 1778 and 1787 and probably extended no further than 1784. Langshaw had sent his son, John Langshaw, Jr., known as Jack, to study music in London under Benjamin Cooke, organist of Westminster Abbey, but the young pupil was dissatisfied with Cooke and turned to the hymn-writer's son, Charles Wesley, Jr., for instruction. The majority of the letters from these years were written by Charles Wesley to John Langshaw. Three were from Langshaw, two of them addressed to Wesley and the other to Cooke. One was from Charles Jr. to Jack Langshaw, The second period extended from 1822 until 1827, during which Charles Wesley, Jr., wrote five letters to Jack Langshaw, who had succeeded his father as organist at Lancaster. The remaining item in this edition was written in 1809 by the hymn-writer's younger son, Samuel Wesley, to Jack Langshaw.

Members of the Langshaw family held the position of organist at Lancaster for fifty-three years. The first of them, John Langshaw (d. 1798),[1] established his reputation as an organ mechanic in the 1760s, when he worked on an instrument for the Earl of Bute that could be used as a barrel organ.[2] In 1772 Langshaw was appointed organist at Lancaster and held the position until his death on March 3, 1798.[3] He had a family of seven children, two of whom died at the age of ten, and another, George, at the age of eighteen.[4] The upbringing of his children was a matter of primary concern for him, and he sent two of his sons to London, Jack for private music lessons and George for education at Charterhouse.

Jack Langshaw (1763-1832) was already in London in September 1778, studying under Benjamin Cooke, when the first of the letters in this collection was written. By November he had discontinued his lessons with Cooke and had transferred to Charles Wesley, Jr., whom he found to be a more satisfactory teacher. Jack returned to Lancaster in the summer of 1779 and did not go to London again until the winter of 1780-1781.[5] He went back to Lancaster in July 1781[6] and in November 1783 Charles Wesley affirmed that he would be glad to welcome Jack.[7] By February 1784 Jack was in London again, and in May of that year he was planning to return home.[8] Jack succeeded his father as organist at Lancaster on April 8, 1798 and held the post until his death on December 5, 1832. It was during this period that a new organ was installed in the church. In 1823, in order to supplement his salary, he applied to Robert Peel, at that time Home Secretary, for appointment as Collector of Stamps for the Hundred of Lonsdale,[9] but it is not known if his application was successful. Jack Langshaw was also a composer, an activity that he began in his youth,[10] but only a few of his works were published.[11]

Although he did not write any of the letters in this collection, Jack Langshaw is the one person who figures in all of them. His musical education was the reason for the correspondence between his father and Charles Wesley and for the letter that his father wrote to Benjamin Cooke; and he was the recipient of the letters from Wesley's two sons.

The third member of the family to become organist at Lancaster was Jack's son, James Pearson Langshaw. This appointment was only for two years, from Easter 1833 to Easter 1835. The Vestry Minutes record that the vicar appointed him for that length of time "solely in consideration of the circumstances in which it is represented the late Organist Mr. John Langshaw has left his Family." At the end of the two years the young organist relinquished the position. Later in life he qualified as a surgeon and played a leading part in the life of Lancaster.

Lancaster is a historic town. Its Priory and Parish Church of St. Mary was originally attached to a religious order, and from the fifteenth century until the Reformation its living was in the presentation of an abbess of the Brigittines. The church stands in an imposing position on a hill overlooking the River Lune, only a few miles from the coast, and near to both the Lake District and the Pennines. Lancaster is over two hundred miles from London, and when Jack Langshaw went to the capital city for his musical education, he encountered through his contact with the Wesley family a world far different from the one that he had previously known.

Charles Wesley (1707-88), the hymn-writer and the author of most of the letters in this edition, was in his seventies when he corresponded with John Langshaw. In 1771 Wesley and his family moved from Bristol to London, Mrs. Gumley gave him the lease of her house in Chesterfield Street, Marylebone, and he resided there until his death on March 29, 1788. During this period his sons grew to manhood and began to establish their musical reputation.

Although he did not profess to be a musician, Wesley probably played a little on the flute in his younger days, and his wife Sarah was reputed to be a fine singer. It was in her, according to her husband, that the musical genius of the family had its origin.[12] That genius flowered in her sons, Charles Jr. (1757-1834) and Samuel (1766-1837), and her grandson, Samuel Sebastian Wesley (1810-76), all of whom were professional musicians.

In these letters Charles Wesley appears primarily as a family man, interested in the welfare of his sons and proud of their accomplishments. He was hospitable, opening his home to Jack Langshaw and other members of that family who were in London. He was knowledgeable about the musical life of London and was already provoking criticism because of the company that he kept. In 1771 John Fletcher, Vicar of Madeley and a leading Methodist, told him, "You have your *enemies* as well as your brother, they complain of your *love for musick, company, fine people, great folks,* and of the *want of your former zeal and frugality*. I need not put you in mind to cut off *sinful appearances. You were taught to do* this before I knew anything of the matter."[13] In 1775 Fletcher later commented, "You are in danger from music, children, poetry; and I from speculation, controversy, sloth, &c., &c. Let us watch against the deceitfulness of self and sin in all their appearances."[14]

Charles Wesley himself had an ambivalent attitude to his sons' involvement in a musical career. He was proud of their achievements and organized concerts for them; yet he refused to let Charles Jr. be educated at the Chapel Royal and discouraged him from applying for an appointment at court. He was suspicious of "the whole Tribe of Musicians" and criticized them for their neglect of Sunday worship and their lack of punctuality.[15]

Wesley took a leading part in publicizing his sons' abilities. Even before they started their series of concerts, they performed to visitors at Chesterfield Street. Most of the guests belonged to the upper echelons of society. Among those who heard the young Wesleys were the Lord Chancellor, the Archbishop of Canterbury, the Bishops of London, Oxford, Durham, Chester, Bristol, and Rochester, and a large number of lords and ladies, as well as Dr. Johnson and Mr. (presumably David) Garrick.[16]

In 1779 Wesley helped to organize the first of the series of concerts. One of the rooms in his house at Chesterfield Street was spacious enough for the performances, and he left notes containing details of these occasions.[17] Seven concerts were held at fortnightly intervals in each of the years 1779-86. Many of the audiences were subscribers, and the number of subscriptions rose from twenty-four in 1779 to forty-eight in 1781. The highest attendance at any of the performances was fifty-eight. As many as ten instrumentalists and five singers took part, and the instruments included two organs and a harpsichord. Samuel led on the violin. Both brothers played the organ, and often they joined each other in organ duets. The music included works by Handel, Purcell, Corelli, Geminiani, and compositions and extemporizations by the Wesley brothers.

An élite group of people attended the concerts. Among them were the poet William Cowper, Daines Barrington, and James Oglethorpe, first governor of Georgia, whom Charles Wesley served as secretary during his brief stay in the colony. The list of those present, like that in 1777, included bishops and members of the aristocracy. One of the subscribers, the Earl of Mornington, father of the Duke of Wellington, was a composer himself and sometimes took part in the performances.[18] John Wesley was present on January 29, 1784,[19] and also attended on January 25, 1781, when he wrote in his *Journal*, "I spent an agreeable hour at a concert of my nephews. But I was a little out of my element among Lords and Ladies. I love plain music and plain company best."

Charles and John Wesley disagreed with each other about the propriety of these concerts. In a letter to John on April 23, 1779, Charles wrote, "I am clear, without a doubt, that my sons concert is after the will and order of Providence. It has established them as musicians, and in a safe and honourable way." After Charles's death John Wesley printed this letter in the *Arminian Magazine* and commented, "I am 'clear' of another mind."[20]

The concerts also provoked criticism from John Wesley's trusted associate, Thomas Coke, although he soon changed his mind. "I looked upon the Concerts," he wrote, "which he allows his sons to have in his own house, to be highly dishono-rable to God; and himself to be criminal, by reason of his situation in the Church of Christ: but on mature consideration of all the circumstances appertaining to them, I cannot now blame him."[21]

Several letters in this edition mention the concerts.[22] "They dont expect to get by it much more than Reputation and increase of Skill," Charles Wesley wrote on December 22, 1781. "I need not tell you the hearts of the Professors towards them. Yet I dont wish them to make more haste to be rich. What more ought we to wish than Content with food & raiment." And on November 4, 1783, Wesley expressed uncertainty about the future of the performances: "I am quite weary of our Concerts, and have a right to spend my last days in peace and quiet." In fact, however, the concerts continued for another three seasons.

During these final years of the hymn-writer's life he was surrounded by his family. His wife and three children were at home with him, and the concerts brought a large number of people to the house. Moreover, he extended hospitality to Jack Langshaw and his brother George. Yet on June 2, 1779, he gave the impression of being a lonely man, complaining that John Langshaw was the only person who corresponded with him.

Wesley was very conscious of the fleeting nature of human life. Even in his earlier years he had expressed the expectation that he would soon die. Now his age and his health gave him added reason to assume that his life would not last much longer. Moreover, he was afraid of an invasion by the French and Spanish, who had formed an alliance with the American Patriots against Britain. "Jack will miss our Concert in the winter," he wrote on July 17,1779, "if we live so long. Who knows what this Summer may bring forth? The King gives us fair warning: but we have long had reason to fear 'This is the Nation to be visited.' I doubt whether the Blow will be any more turned aside." His fears extended to his family, and on October 26, 1779, he raised doubts that Charles Jr. would survive until the next summer.

Wesley's letters quickly and easily move from comments on the details of everyday life to reflections on the ways and purposes of God. He was confident of a life beyond the grave and strong in his assurance of divine providence. "Why else have we met on earth," he asked in a postscript to Langshaw on May 17, 1779, "but that we may spend an happy Eternity together?" "I have five children waiting for me in one grave," he wrote on June 5, 1782. "The days of our mourning will soon be ended." This experience of bereavement enabled him to understand Langshaw's feelings at the death of his son, George.

The letters by Wesley, like his hymns, abound with scriptural phrases and allusions. They also contain echoes of his own hymns and the Book of Common Prayer. They show his familiarity with English literature and make allusions to Milton, Shakespeare, and Addison. Of special interest are four quotations from the poet Edward Young (1683-1765), whose work is now largely forgotten. Young's poems had many admirers in the eighteenth century, and his *Night Thoughts* led Charles Wesley to write in his *Journal* for July 30, 1754, "No writings but the inspired are more useful to me."[23]

In this correspondence Wesley showed how fully he shared his brother John's opposition to the American Revolution. He expressed agreement with the American Loyalist, Joseph Galloway, who urged the British government to be more aggressive in waging the war.[24] But his patriotism did not prevent him from reacting with fear to the possibility that Charles Jr. and Jack Langshaw might be pressed into military service (July 23, 1781?).

Wesley's political sympathies were for the king. After Britain's defeat at Yorktown, he was deeply concerned about the fate of the Loyalists in America, and in 1784 he declared his support for George III and William Pitt, the Younger, whom the king had appointed Prime Minister at the end of the previous year. When Pitt successfully resisted his political opposition, Wesley commented, "The Lovers of his Majesty rejoice in the late Defeat of his Enemies" (March 1784).

References to Methodism are sparse in this correspondence. Charles Wesley was increasingly dissatisfied with the direction that the movement was taking and feared that it would eventually separate from the Church of England. In a letter to Langshaw he emphasized his Anglican rather than his Methodist connections. "You need not fear our making Jack a Methodist," he wrote on April 6, 1779. "I dont wish my own Children to be so called. God, I trust, will make them Christians that is, Sound Members of the Church of England." Another important mention of the Methodist movement in this correspondence is Wesley's assurance that his brother's followers are loyal supporters of George III (March 1784).

Charles shared his brother John's partiality for early rising, a habit which he advocated for Jack Langshaw. Although in his prime Wesley had risen at four, he was content to prescribe five o'clock for Jack. "Let him go to bed at Ten & rise at 5. - all the year round. - I had rather leave my Children such an Habit than an Estate" (May 17, 1779).[25] But Wesley later relented and conceded that six would be an acceptable hour (September 25, 1780).

The correspondence reflects Wesley's interest in the musical life of London. He speaks with sorrow of the deaths of William Boyce and Joseph Kelway.[26] He compares the fees charged by the leading teachers of music in London.[27] And he expresses his disapproval of Benjamin Cooke. It was not only clergymen who held more than one position at the same time. Pluralism extended to organists. Wesley was critical of Cooke for wanting to hold appointments at both Westminster Abbey and St. Martin-in-the-Fields.[28] But he spoke no ill of Boyce, who had also been organist of two churches concurrently.

Six of the letters in the collection were written by Charles Wesley, Jr., the eldest surviving child of the hymn-writer, who was born in Bristol on December 11, 1757. Musically Charles Jr. was an infant prodigy and could play by ear on the harpsichord before he was three years old. At first his father did not encourage him to pursue a musical education and declined an opportunity to send him to the Chapel Royal. When the family moved to London, the young Charles took lessons from Joseph Kelway, organist at St. Martin-in-the-Fields, and from William Boyce, one of the most distinguished English composers of that time, who was organist of the Chapel Royal and Master of the King's Music. By the time he was twenty years old Charles Wesley, Jr., was taking pupils, and Jack Langshaw was one of them. He used the lesson books of Handel and Scarlatti in teaching Jack and encouraged him to practice composition. As well as performing in the concerts at his parents' home, Charles Jr. appeared before royalty, playing for the Prince Regent at Brighton, King George III at Windsor, and Princess Charlotte at Warwick House. In 1788 he declined to apply for the position of organist at the Chapel Royal, out of respect for the wishes of his father, who feared that the influence of court life might be detrimental to him. Charles Jr. probably regretted this decision and on several later occasions sent letters to royalty, asking for their assistance in obtaining an appointment.[29] Although he continued to play at court, he applied unsuccessfully for several positions as organist, including that at St. Paul's Cathedral. Eventually he obtained appointments at the chapel of the Lock Hospital and later at St. Marylebone Parish Church, where he remained until his death on May 23, 1834.[30] St. Marylebone Church was an ancient foundation. A large new building was erected there in 1817, and a fine organ was built in the church. Marylebone was the neighborhood in which Charles Wesley's family had resided ever since 1771. After the hymn-writer's death his widow lived there with their three children. Samuel soon went his separate way, but Charles Jr. and Sally remained at home.

Charles Jr.'s letters in this collection were written to Jack Langshaw. He probably wrote the first in 1784 when Jack had returned to Lancaster after completing his training in London. The other five come from the 1820s, when Charles Jr. and Jack Langshaw were exchanging information about each other's compositions and Charles was assisting Jack in his attempt to publish his arrangement of work by Corelli and Geminiani. The letters give insights into the musical life of London. They contain references to the organ-builders, John Gray, William Allen, Benjamin Blyth, and Henry Cephas Lincoln, and to the publishers Thomas Preston and Robert Birchall. They mention Gertrud-Elisabeth Mara, Elizabeth Billington, and James Bartleman, who were well known singers of the time. They speak of the places where concerts were held, the Hanover Square Rooms and Covent Garden. And they allude to numerous composers ranging from Corelli and Geminiani to Thomas Attwood, an English contemporary of Charles Wesley, Jr.

The correspondence gives a picture of life in the Wesley family. Charles Jr. tells of his mother Sarah's death at the end of 1822 and often speaks of his sister Sally, whose health appeared to be failing and who died in 1828, a year after the writing of the last of the letters in this collection. He writes of the music that he and his brother composed, and reveals his displeasure at the new Rector of St. Marylebone's opposition to the use of organ voluntaries in worship (November 1, 1825). And he alludes to the reconstruction of the St. Marylebone organ by Gray in 1826 and the removal of a large painting by Benjamin West from its place behind the altar (January 11, 1827).

Charles Jr. did not fulfil his early promise. In his later years his reputation as an organist was not as great as his brother Samuel's, and his compositions did not make a lasting impact. He wrote much of his music in the earlier part of his life, publishing five string quartets (about 1778), six concertos for organ or harpsichord (about 1780), eight songs (1784), and a Concerto Grosso (1784). He also wrote a Second Grand Concerto (c.1784), music for Mason's *Caractacus* (1791) and an oratorio, *Elijah*, as well as various anthems, organ works, and few hymn tunes.

The musical taste of Charles Jr. was somewhat conservative. He was a frequent attender at the Concerts of Ancient (Antient) Music, which on principle did not include music less than twenty years old. Among his favorite composers were Handel, Scarlatti, and Geminiani, and he had a high opinion of Boyce, in whose memory he set to music an ode written by Charles Wesley. His early compositions, while they contain echoes of earlier styles, are examples of the "galant" style that reached its zenith in Haydn and Mozart.[31] Charles Jr.'s letters give the impression that he was not in sympathy with more recent fashions in music,[32] and in his later years he ceased to attend the performances of oratorios in London.[33]

Samuel Wesley, the younger surviving son of the hymn-writer, was the author of one of the letters in this collection, in which he recommended Thomas Elliot as builder for the proposed organ at the Lancaster church, a recommendation that was not accepted. He was a more distinguished composer than his brother, and some of his works are still in the repertoire of church choirs and organists. He was born in Bristol on February 24, 1766. Like his brother, he showed himself a natural musician from an early age and was a teenager in the years when he performed in the concerts at his home. In 1784, much to the distress of his father, he became a Roman Catholic, but later he reverted to Anglicanism. He was influential in introducing the works of Johann Sebastian Bach into England and, together with Karl Friedrich Horn, published editions of Bach's *Organ Trios* and *Well-tempered Clavier*.

Although he did not have a position at a church, Samuel Wesley had a high reputation as an organist. He was well-known as a lecturer on musical topics. He composed numerous works, including symphonies, oratorios, organ concertos, and many motets, among the best known of which are "Dixit

Dominus," "Exultate Deo," and "In Exitu Israel." As well as writing hymn tunes of his own, in 1826 he discovered three tunes in the Fitzwilliam Library, Cambridge, which Handel had composed for hymns by Charles Wesley.[34]

Samuel married Charlotte Louisa Martin in 1793. They were soon separated but never divorced, and for the last twenty-eight years of his life Samuel lived with Sarah Suter. He died in 1837 and was interred in St. Marylebone old churchyard, the burial place of his parents and his brother. The eldest son of Samuel's union with Sarah Suter was Samuel Sebastian Wesley (1810-76), who won fame as an organist and composer of church music in the mid nineteenth century and whose work is better known than that of either his father or his uncle.

Although Samuel Wesley is the author of one of these letters and is mentioned in several of them, the collection is chiefly concerned with the two Charles Wesleys and the two John Langshaws. It gives a glimpse of the daily lives and interests of the Langshaws and their sorrows and successes. Above all, it provides information about Charles Wesley and his elder son. It reveals the thoughts, feelings, and faith of the hymn-writer in the later period of his life, giving insight into his attitude to affairs of both church and state, and providing evidence of his devotion to his sons. It is a source of evidence about the activities and aspirations of Charles Wesley, Jr., at two different stages of his life, the first when he was taking part in the concerts in Chesterfield Street, and the second when he was organist at St. Marylebone. In later life, both as a composer and an organist, he lived under the shadow of his younger and more talented brother Samuel. But although he was not a star in England's musical firmament, he had numerous acquaintances in musical circles. His letters offer an interesting portrait of the man himself and of the society in which he moved.

The correspondence in this edition provides important information on a variety of topics. It gives evidence of the activities and attitudes of Charles Wesley during the final decade of his life, and it sheds light on the Wesley family, especially Charles Jr. It gives an insight into the life of the provincial organists John and Jack Langshaw. It also supplies evidence of the activities of other British musicians of the period. It tells of their ambitions, rivalries, and friendships, and opens a window on to that distant world of music.

The Text of the Correspondence

Most of the letters from the Wesleys to the Langshaws are arranged so that the address is on the back when the letter is folded. Many of them also have a postmark, but the three letters from John Langshaw (Letters 1, 2, and 7) have neither address nor postmark on the back, and appear to be drafts of the letters that Langshaw sent. It is clear that the present collection was made by the Langshaw family.

In addition to the letters from Langshaw, Letters 22 and 23 have no address on the back, and Letters 17, 18, 19, 20, 21, 22, 23, 24, 25, 26, 27, 32, and 33 have no postmark. Since Letters 3 and 14 have a later date than the postmark, Charles Wesley dated them erroneously. Letter 9 has an earlier date than the postmark, presumably because Wesley mailed it the day after he wrote it.[35] Most of the letters also have a date written on the back, always in the same handwriting, presumably that of the collector.

The spelling, capitalization, and punctuation of the letters has been for the most part reproduced, except that the majority of abbreviated words are printed in full, and the superscript has not been preserved in the abbreviations that remain. Abbreviations have been expanded as follows: affect^e - affectionate; ans^d - answered; Bp - Bishop; Bro^r - Brother; Covnt - Covent; f^m - from; his M., H.M. - His Majesty; L^d - Lord; L^r - Letter; MS^t, M.S.^{t} - Manuscript; M^{rs} -Masters; obed^t - obedient; o^r - our; Ora^o - Oratorio; sch - school; Servt - Servant; sh^d - shoud; Sq^{re} - Square; S^r - Sir; w^{ch} - which; w^d - woud; Xn'd - Christened; y^e -the; y^m - them; Y^r, Y^{rs} - Your, Yours; y^t - that. The abbreviations "sh^d" and "w^d" in Charles Wesley's letters have been expanded to "shoud" and "woud", the spelling that he normally used. Punctuation after "Mr", "Mrs", and "Dr" has been regularized. In the explanatory notes, however, the punctuation of the addresses on the back of the letters has been preserved.

It is not always clear whether a stop is a comma or a period (full stop), and an editorial decision has been made without comment. When the last letter of a sentence ends with a flourish, and on a few other occasions, a period (full stop) has been silently inserted into the text. Several sentences, especially in the items by Charles Wesley, Jr., begin with lower-case letters, and they have been silently changed to capitals.

Spellings have only rarely been altered, and a note indicates where such changes have been made. For the most part obsolete spellings have been preserved, e.g., acknowlege, allways, aprobation, arived, beleive, capasities, coppied, expence, harpsicord, mentain, peices, plauged (for "plagued"), sence, somthing, somtime, surprize, and whither (for "whether"). Obsolete or mistaken spellings of proper names have not usually been changed, e.g., Albermarle, Britanicus, Burchall. Even if there is no evidence for a spelling in the Oxford English Dictionary, it has usually been transcribed, e.g., consumpsion, entirly, erisipolis, frequant, reccomend. In a few cases, where the writer has obviously omitted a letter, it has been editorially inserted, as in "Libra<r>ies" and "lik<e>wise. Apostrophes in plural nouns, such as "Concerto's" and "Oratorio's," and in the present tense of verbs, such as "tell's," have been silently deleted. Words underlined in the manuscript have been italicized. Ampersands and the abbreviation &c (etc.) have been retained.

The dates on the cover in an unknown hand are not recorded unless there is a discrepancy about the date.

Signs Used in Textual Notes

    [ ]   deletion in text

    ∧ ∧   interlinear or marginal insertion

    < >   editorial insertion or conjecture

    /   end of line marker

Insertions are always interlinear unless otherwise stated. For example, Letter 1, note 3 (Text: [takes] ∧first∧) indicates that Langshaw deleted *takes* and made the interlinear insertion *first took*. If an insertion or conjecture is made by the editor, this change is noted and the signs < > are used. When an incomplete word has been deleted, an editorial conjecture is sometimes made about the word that the correspondent intended to write. For example, Letter 12, note 8 (Text: Six, [or F<ive>]), indicates that Wesley wrote "Six," began to add "or Five" but deleted the addition before he had completed the second word. In Letter 2, note 3 (Text: [on<ly>] playing only) indicates that Langshaw began to write "only" but deleted it before he had finished the word, and then wrote "playing only". But neither of the last two words was interlinear.

* * * *

Letter 15 in this collection is transcribed from the original in the Methodist Collection, Drew University Library. All the other letters are transcribed from originals in the John Wesley Collection, Special Collections Department, Robert W. Woodruff Library, Emory University.

Biblical references are to the Authorized (King James) Version, except where it is indicated that reference is made to the version of the Psalms in the Book of Common Prayer.

❧— INTRODUCTION NOTES —❧

[1] The family gravestone in the grounds of the Lancaster church records that Langshaw died on March 3, 1798 at the age of 73, implying that he was born in either 1724 or 1725. *DNB*, however, gives 1718 as the date of his birth, and F. J. Fétis, ed., *Biographie universelle des musiciens*, 2nd ed. (Paris: Firmin Didot, 1870), says that it was about 1718. Cf. *Grove*[3].

[2] See Letter 32, note 18.

[3] William Oliver Roper, ed., *Materials for the History of the Church of Lancaster* (Remains Historical and Literary connected with the Palatine Counties of Lancaster and Chester, New Series, 26, 31, 58, 59), 4 vols. (Manchester: Chetham Society, 1892-1906), 3:637; 4:780. According to George T. O. Bridgeman, *The History of the Church & Manor of Wigan* (Remains, New Series, 15-18), 4 vols. (Manchester: Chetham Society, 1888-89), 3:636, John Langshaw was organist of Wigan Parish Church from 1770 to 1772. But W. J. True, *A Ramble Round Wigan Parish Church*, rev. ed. (Wigan: Thomas Wall and Sons, 1924), 103, 121, describes the Wigan organist both as John and as William Langshaw. John Langshaw may have made additions to the organ of Trinity Church, Kendal, and been a member of the barrel-organ firm, "White and Langshaw." Boeringer, 2:95; 3:287; Noel Boston and Lyndesay G. Langwill, *Church and Chamber Barrel-Organs* (Edinburgh: Lyndesay G. Langwill, 1967), 62, 70; Arthur W. J. G. Ord-Hume, *Barrel Organ* (London: George Allen & Unwin; South Brunswick and New York: A. S. Barnes and Co., 1978), 250, 462, 489.

[4] See Letter 1, note 7.

[5] See Letters 11, 12, and 16.

[6] See Letters 17, 18, note 1, and 19.

[7] Letter 23.

[8] Letters 24 and 26. Jack was present at the Wesley concerts in February, March, and April, 1784. See RAM, Wesley, 77, 79, 81-83, 85.

[9] John Langshaw, Jr., to Robert (later Sir Robert) Peel, February 1, 1823, BL, Add. MS. 40,354, fol. 138r-v.

[10] Boeringer, 2:95, suggests that Jack, like his father, may have been active in the firm of "White and Langshaw".

[11] Jack Langshaw's publications included several songs, arrangements for duet of choruses by Handel and Haydn, and a theme with variations for pianoforte or harp. John S. Sainsbury, *A Dictionary of Music and Musicians from the Earliest Times*. 2 vols. (London: Sainsbury, 1825; reprint, New York: Da Capo Press, 1971); *DNB*. See also Letter 29, note 2.

[12] Reminiscences of Samuel Wesley, BL, Add. MS. 27,593, 9.

[13] John Fletcher to Charles Wesley, October 13, 1771, Woodruff.

[14] John Fletcher to Charles Wesley, January 1775, *Letters of the Rev. John Fletcher*, ed. Melville Horne (New York: Lane & Scott, 1849), 261.

[15] Letters 8 and 14. Many years earlier Charles Wesley had written:
>Still let us on our guard be found,
> And watch against the power of sound
>   With sacred jealousy;
>Lest haply sense should damp our zeal,
> And music's charms bewitch and steal
>   Our heart away from thee.

Hymns and Sacred Poems, 2 vols. (Bristol: Farley, 1749), 2:255-56; Franz Hildebrandt and Oliver A. Beckerlegge, eds., *A Collection of Hymns for the Use of The People Called Methodists, The Works of John Wesley*, 7 (Nashville: Abingdon Press, 1983): 327.

16 "Hearers of Chas & Sam 1777," MARC, Charles Wesley Black Folio 4:59.

17 Wesley's notes for 1779-85 are in the Library of the Royal Academy of Music (MS. GB: Lam MS-L WESLEY, C). A copy made by his granddaughter Eliza Wesley is in the British Library (BL, Add. MS. 38,071), and several notes in Wesley's own hand are in the Methodist Archives and Research Centre, John Rylands University Library of Manchester, including records for 1786 (MARC, Charles Wesley Black Folio 4:52, 55-58).

18 Samuel Wesley, BL, Add. MS. 27,593. Mornington was reputed to be a distant cousin of the Wesleys, but scholars now question this tradition. NG.

19 For a discussion of the concerts see F. G. Edwards, "Samuel Wesley, 1766-1837," *Musical Times* 43 (August, 1902): 525-28; W. W. (William Wallace?), "The Wesley Family Concerts: 1779-1785," *The R. A. M. Club Magazine* 84 (June 1929):7-11.

20 *Arminian Magazine* 12 (1789): 387.

21 Thomas Coke to John Wesley, December 15, 1779 (*Arminian Magazine* 13 [1790]: 50-51).

22 Letters 6, 8, 11, 13, 15, 20, 23, and 24 by Charles Wesley, and Letter 7 by John Langshaw.

23 Letters 11, 12, and 22. *The Journal of the Rev. Charles Wesley, M.A.*, edited by Thomas Jackson, 2 vols. (London: John Mason, 1849), 2:106. Young influenced the language of Charles Wesley's hymns. See *Collection of Hymns, passim*, and Index, 848.

24 Letters 19 and 20, September 28 and December 22, 1781.

25 Letter 9. See also Letters 12 and 14.

26 Letters 8 and 21.

27 Letter 14.

28 Letter 21.

29 James T. Lightwood, *Samuel Wesley, Musician: The Story of his Life* (London: Epworth Press, 1937), 71, 74; Frank Baker, *Charles Wesley: As Revealed by His Letters* (London: Epworth Press, 1948), 114.

30 Samuel Wesley, BL, Add. MS. 27,593. A manuscript by G. P. England indicates that Charles Jr. had a salary of a hundred pounds a year at St. Marylebone Church (Boeringer, 2:324).

31 See Gerald Finzi's comments in Charles Wesley (Jr.), *Easy String Quartets*. ed. Gerald Finzi, Hinrichsen Edition, Nos. 411-416 (London: Hinrichsen, 1953). See also the introduction to Charles Wesley (Jr.), *Concerto No. 4 in C major for Pianoforte (Harpsichord or Organ), String orchestra (2 Violins, Viola, V'cello-Cb); and Oboes ad lib.*, ed. and arr. Gerald Finzi, Hinrichsen Edition No. 290 (London: Hinrichsen, 1956).

32 Letters 29 and 30, October 17, 1822, and April 3, 1823.

33 Letter 30, April 3, 1823.

34 See Letter 33, January 11, 1827, notes 4 and 5.

35 For a discussion of letter seals, addresses, postmarks, and the folding of sheets, see Frank Baker's Introduction to John Wesley, *Letters, I, The Works of John Wesley*, 25 (Oxford: Clarendon Press, 1980): 68-78.

THE CORRESPONDENCE

JOHN LANGSHAW TO CHARLES WESLEY
SEPTEMBER 28, 1778[1]

Dear Sir,

    I have received several agreeable letters from my Son, giving an account of the very kind reception he meets with at your house. The poor boy has been no little mortified at the method Dr. Cook[2] first took[3] with him, & if it was not for the prospect he has of better success from Mr. Charles,[4] I should find it difficult to keep him quiet under the Doctor.[5] Your kindness to the lad comes at a very seasonable time, as things happen: I wish I may be able to requite you; somthing I will do, & what I cannot, I must leave to my Son, for a future day.

    Jack is the oldest of seven Children,[6] & he but fifteen last February.[7] All my hopes are on him to support my Wife & little ones if I fall while they are helpless; therefore I must make hast to get the boy well, & speedily instructed; & I must make use of my friends; as a hundred a year[8] (the utmost I get) will not both mentain my large[9] family, & pay the high fees some Masters demand.[10]

    Jack sends me word, that[11] Mr. Charles has promised to teach him Handels old Lessons: Nothing could have hit my wishes better than that design. I would sooner chuse the boy to be taught those lessons, Scarlattis[12] or[13] Kelways,[14] by Mr. Charles, than by any other Master in the kingdom; for besides his own good abilities, he has had the assistance of the best player[15] of that Musick in England. And[16] whoever can play Handel's, Scarlatti's, & Kelway's Lessons; has nothing to fear from any other author.

    No man in this County can play Handel's Lessons, nor have we one capable of teaching them.

    This letter is to give you our[17] hearty thanks for your kindness, to my boy; & our[18] compliments to Mrs. Wesley,[19] Mr. Charles, & his Brother & Sister.[20]

When you see Mr. Green,²¹ if you'll tell him I am well, & often think of him; that information will be as acceptable²² to him, as the old form²³ of *Compliments*, & will oblige your most obedient Servant.

J L.

To the Revd. Mr. C. Wesley.
Sept. 28. 1778.

⸺ LETTER NO. 1 NOTES ⸺

[1] John Langshaw complains of the tuition that his son, Jack, has received from Benjamin Cooke and looks forward to the prospect of Jack's receiving lessons from Charles Wesley, Jr.

[2] Benjamin Cooke (1734-93), organist of Westminster Abbey from 1762 and of St. Martin-in-the-Fields from 1782. *DNB*; *NG*; Shaw, 334-35.

[3] Text: [takes] ∧first took∧

[4] Charles Wesley, Jr.

[5] Text: Docter *altered to* Doctor

[6] Text: ∧Children,∧

[7] The other Langshaw children included George (d.1782 at the age of 18), William (b. 1772), James (1773-84), Joseph (bapt. 1775, d. 1785), and Benjamin (bapt. 1775).

[8] A hundred pounds a year.

[9] Text: ∧large∧

[10] For fees charged by teachers in London see Letters 4 and 14.

[11] Text: ∧that∧

[12] Domenico Scarlatti (1685-1757), composer and harpsichord virtuoso, had a great influence on the techniques of performance and composition. *NG*.

[13] Text: [&] ∧or∧

[14] Joseph Kelway (c.1702-1782), organist and harpsichord player, was organist of St. Michael's, Cornhill, and St. Martin-in-the-Fields. He was one of Charles Jr.'s teachers and a pupil of Geminiani. *DNB*; *NG*.

[15] Kelway.

[16] Text: [And] [&] ∧And∧

[17] Text: [my] ∧our∧

[18] Text: [to give my] ∧our∧

[19] Sarah Wesley, née Gwynne (1726-1822), married Charles in 1749.

[20] Sarah (Sally) Wesley (1759-1828).

[21] Samuel Green, the organ builder (1740-96). See Letter 29, note 10.

[22] Text: [instead of] ∧as acceptable∧

[23] Text: fo∧r∧m

JOHN LANGSHAW TO BENJAMIN COOKE
SEPTEMBER 28, 1778[1]

Dear Sir,

By my Sons letters, I understand that he is very[2] often at your house, & that you hear him play Harpsicord lessons. The boy is keen set upon being a good player, for he knows that playing only[3] is regarded in this Country; yet[4] I could wish he would[5] have somthing in his head as well as his fingers, as he has now so good an advantage of getting that sort of instruction; but as he is so set upon playing, it will fret[6] him to take him from[7] it. I think you have found out his temper, for he tells me, he has your good opinion, The lad is desirous of[8] learning, & of an open free temper, but hard words are too much for him; he will do his utmost for a word of aprobation, & I am glad you give it him. I shall shortly have an opportunity of sending you half a years pay for Jack, it will but[9] poorly requite you for your frequant trouble with him, but if we have it in our power you shall be better rewarded.

I desire my kind respects to my good Friend Sir John Hawkins[10] when you see him and am Your most obedient & obliged Servant.

JL:

To Dr. Cook
Sept. 28.- 78.

⎯⎯ LETTER NO. 2 NOTES ⎯⎯

1 For Cooke see Letter 1, note 2.
2 Text: [very] ∧is∧ ver[r]y
3 Text: [on<ly>] playing only
4 Text: yet *written over an indecipherable deletion.*
5 Text: [might] ∧would∧
6 Text: [hurt] ∧fret∧
7 Text: [of] ∧from∧
8 Text: [free] [willing to] ∧desirous of∧
9 Text: ∧but∧
10 Sir John Hawkins (1719-89), author of *The General History of the Science and Practice of Music* (1776). He wrote a life of Samuel Johnson, that was outclassed by Boswell's. *DNB*; *NG*.

CHARLES WESLEY TO JOHN LANGSHAW
OCTOBER 21 (22), 1778[1]

Chesterfield street
Marybone[2] Oct. 22
1778

My dear Sir,

My Son thinks himself happy, that it is in his power to assist a worthy Friend. You woud be glad to shew the like kindness to me, or mine. Your Son I bear a Paternal Regard to. Charles has begun teaching him Scarlatti's Music[3], which he catches with surprizing Quickness. Handel Kelway, Geminiani[4] follow - as he is ready for them.

I know not what you pay the Doctor[5] for his Instructions: but as a Friend, I must inform you. *He is generally thought to know a great deal of Music; but not to have the Talent of Communicating his knowledge.* Your Son's board, I hope, costs you little.

I have given him a piece of important Advice. To go to bed & rise *early*: which I wish you to inforce. He has not yet got our acquaintance in London. Let him stand to this wise Resolution, & he is safe. He is already a Favourite of my whole Family, who love him for his Sense & Modesty. - My Wife unites in wishing you & your Companion & children all happiness in both worlds. A Letter from you will be always acceptable to,

dear Sir,
Your very affectionate Servant
C Wesley.

LETTER NO. 3 NOTES

1. Address: Mr Langshaw/ Organist/ Lancaster.
   Postmark: 21 OC
   Wesley's date, October 22, is mistaken.
2. *Marybone* presumably indicates how Wesley pronounced "Marylebone."
3. Text: Scarlatti∧'s Music∧
4. Francesco Geminiani (c.1687-1762), composer and violinist, a pupil of Corelli, and a teacher of Kelway. *NG*.
5. Benjamin Cooke.

4

CHARLES WESLEY TO JOHN LANGSHAW
NOVEMBER 16, 1778[1]

London
Nov. 16. 1778

Dear Sir,

The Doctors think the Trade overstocked: therefore you must not expect They woud multiply Masters.[2] Dr. W.[3] had half a guinea[4] a Lesson from every *future* Organist. Dr. Boyce[5] the same: & he well deserved it. Dr.—'s[6] Terms woud be very reasonable indeed, if he had really *intended* to make your Son Master of his art. Ten pound is too much to pay for Nothing.

Charles has appointed him to come for instruction twice a Week; which will be sufficient to set him up for a Country Organist[7] in One year; if he can take advice, & strictly follow Charles's Directions. One only Condition I propose, Namely that he shall rise early, & study regularly. On the Evening which he spends with us every week, he may hear the most excellent Music: which will be full as useful to him, as playing himself. But both my Sons will help him forward:- if he continues sober diligent and teachable. His success, you see, depends principally upon himself.

Charles will find him constant employment and carry him on & as fast as he himself chuses.

Direct your Letters to me at the Foundery[8] but not Post paid. I shall be always glad to hear of yours & your family's welfare: for you may safely beleive me,

dear Sir,
Your affectionate Servant
& Friend
C Wesley.

LETTER NO. 4 NOTES

[1] Address: Mr Langshaw/Organist/Lancaster
Postmark: Only NO is visible.
On the cover is the stamp "POST PAID" and another stamp "Post paid." with the written entry "4d" (four pence).

[2] Doctors are musicians with a university doctorate. Masters are recognized teachers of music but not necessarily university graduates.

[3] John Worgan (1724-90), organist and composer. He recognized Charles Jr.'s merits as an infant prodigy, and Charles Jr. played the organ at his funeral. *DNB*; *NG*.

[4] A *guinea* was one pound, one shilling. Half a guinea was ten shillings and sixpence.

[5] William Boyce (bapt. 1711; d. 1779), organist of St. Michael's, Cornhill, All Hallows, Thames Street, and the Chapel Royal, was conductor of the Three Choirs' Festival and Master of the King's Music (1755-79). Boyce, a leading English composer of his day, gave lessons to Charles Jr., and on his death Charles Wesley wrote an ode (*Arminian Magazine* 2 [1779]: 606), which Charles Jr. set to music. *DNB*; *NG*; Shaw, 12-13.

[6] Benjamin Cooke.

[7] An organist outside the London area.

[8] Until the City Road Chapel was built in 1778, the Foundery was the central Methodist place of worship in London.

CHARLES WESLEY TO JOHN LANGSHAW
DECEMBER 24, 1778[1]

London
Dec. 24. 1778

My dear Sir,

You know the Masters too well, to wonder at their Selfishness. My Sons are glad to supply their lack of service & assistance: And your Son is glad to receive instruction. His profiting by it you will be a Judge of at his return.

We thank you for your Present: which, we doubt not, will prove very good when we taste it.

If Charles makes a good Musician of your Son[2] (which there is no reason to doubt of) he[3] has his reward: especially when Jack[4] proves another father to your Family. And as to You -

A grateful mind by owing pays, at once
Indebted & discharg'd.[5]

In your absence I look upon Jack as my adopted Son, & we all love him, as one of the Family. Charles[6] expects to continue five months in town: in which time his Pupil may make a great Progress.

Ought you not to be at a certainty with the Friend he boards with? You will <excuse>[7] the Question as I know you have no great Superfluities. But we know the way to provide all these other things, namely by seeking the kingdom First.[8]

Give[9] <my love when you wait upon him>[10] to your Brother,[11] & be<leive>[12] me his & your very affectionate Servant

C Wesley

LETTER NO. 5 NOTES

1. Address: Mr Lanshaw (sic)/ Organist/ Lancaster
   Postmark: 24 DE
2. Text: ∧Son∧
3. Text: he [∧Jack∧]
4. Text: [he] ∧Jack∧
5. See John Milton, *Paradise Lost,* 4.55-57.
6. Text: [M<r>] Charles
7. Text: ∧<excuse>∧ (*script not clear*)
8. See Matt. 6:33.
9. Text: [Send] ∧Give∧
10. Text: *The script is damaged where the seal was broken.*
11. Langshaw's brother, William. See also Letters 6, 7, 8, 14, 15, 16, 22, and 26, and Introduction, note 3.
12. Text: *The script is damaged where the seal was broken.*

CHARLES WESLEY TO JOHN LANGSHAW
FEBRUARY, 1 1779[1]

London
Febr. 1. 1779

Dear Sir,

Sir J.'s[2] "hard words" shoud give you no disturbance. They are the language of Passion not of Reason. Neither is he *much* to be blamed; as he has not his full Evidence. If he knew all (which it woud not be proper to inform him of) he woud commend Jack's prudent Behaviour.

I charge your Son to take it all patiently, & to hold his tongue, & to mind his business. It is not his business to write to, or expostulate with, a great man.

Charles sets out, as a Master, with a resolution to give his Scholars all the advantages he can. He will not be kind to teach a Dunce, or any person whom he despairs of making a Musician. Your Son is as willing to learn, as He to teach: & pays his Master by his Progress, & good Behaviour. Charles has taken him in to his Concert, which will be of real advantage to him.[3] Before they part, Jack will (we hope) be Master of his Art & Profession.

Return my love to your Brother, who has some hand (tho' he does not know it) in Jack's Instruction. At leaving town he made me a present of a Guinea;[4] (at a time I wanted it) which I have lain it upon Charles, never to forget. My Wife joins me in every kind wish for Mrs. Langshaw yourself & children.

Yours most affectionately
C W.

P.S.
My Father had 19 children; yet never turned away his face from a poor Man. My Eldest Brother brought up all the rest.[5]

⸻ LETTER NO. 6 NOTES ⸺

[1] Address: Mr Langshaw./ Lancaster.
Written on the cover in the unknown hand is "Respecting the dispute with Sir John Hawkins".

[2] Sir John Hawkins. Apparently Hawkins had spoken harshly to Jack for transferring from Cooke to Charles Jr.

[3] One of the concerts given by Charles Jr. and Samuel.

[4] For Langshaw's brother, William, see Letter 5, note 11. For *Guinea* see Letter 4, note 4.

[5] Charles Wesley's father, Samuel, ran into financial difficulties, and his eldest brother, Samuel Jr., gave financial assistance to the family. See also Letters 8 and 13.

7

JOHN LANGSHAW TO CHARLES WESLEY
FEBRUARY 15, 1779

My dear Friend.

 With your last kind letter, I got one from Jack, which begins thus "Mr. Wesleys are indeed the best friends I have got in town,[1] & I hope I shall always continue to deserve it.<"> I hope he always will[2] keep a grateful sence of[3] your goodness to him in his mind. By his letters he seems to be in good spirits, he tells me in this last[4] that he has begun on Handel's 4th lesson, & has got four of Scarlatti's,[5] by some other letters I was informed he had got two of Handel's Concertos[6] in the 3d set, & the 5th & 2d lessons, by this account I am satisfied he is not idle, & that he must be greatly improved, or his[7] Master would not set him to play the 2d & 4th lessons of Handel, which I think are as hard as any in the book. Jack says not a word of his own improvement, nor how much time he spends in practice, I only guess from what he plays, It is your letters give me the most positive information.

 What you tell me of Mr. Charles's aversion to teaching dunces, just answers my opinion. When Jack pressed so to leave the Doctor, I told him you must first be secured, for I had my fears on more accounts than one, but one was, that Mr. Charles might have objections, as it is natural for those Masters[8] of uncommon capasities, to expect somthing of their own likeness[9] in a Scholar;[10] here I feared for Jack; but when I had your consent, & knowing Jack had been tried, I told my Wife I was sure Jack would do, or Mr. C would not be plauged[11] with him. And from Your letters, & what Jack plays I have such hopes as give me great pleasure. I have just wrote to my Brother, & given him as much of your letter as will make him[12] happy. Will: always said you was good natured, I find it so to a great degree.[13] When I was last in London I was desirous of hearing your sons play, but from my own rustick tempers, I had no reason to expect it, but mentioning my *Wishes* & *Fears* to Dr. Worgan, he assured me you would let me hear them, - You did so, & moreover promised they should help Jack, then I was quite amazed, & with great reason. But in every stage of my life I have received good for evil. I could write such things as would to many appear all Romance, or Enthusiasm. What you are doing for Jack, is[14] a continuance of favours I have been receiving ever[15] since I was a boy, with one Eye I looke to the second *Causes* & wish to be grateful, but with another Eye I see the moving[16] first *Cause* of all, but cannot say I am truly[17] thankful.

On this subject I have often strange thoughts.

I am Sorry to see in the News Papers, that Mr. Charles has lost so good a Master: I hope the Doctor has left in his possession a large quantity of his knowlege in Composition, for in that Art I think Dr. Boyce was very great.[18]

Now for whipping[19] between Dr. Worgan & Dr. Cooke, for the King's Plate.[20]

Your Concerts will be of very great service to Jack, so much good playing by his Masters I hope will not be all lost. Jack tells me his Master is for attempting to get a Ticket for Bach & Abel's Concert,[21] & will then go with[22] him, Jack's Master proves a Brother to him.

My Wife joins me in kind thanks to Mrs. Wesley your self and Children for every kindness[23] you shew our Jack.

From Your most obedient & obliged Servant

J L

to the Revd. Mr. Wesley
15 Feb: -79.

⸺ LETTER NO. 7 NOTES ⸺

[1] Text: [London] ∧town∧
[2] Text: [will] always ∧will∧
[3] Text: ∧a grateful sence of∧
[4] Text: [letter] ∧last∧
[5] Text: Scarlatti[e]'s
[6] Text: Concerto[e]s
[7] Text: his *may have been altered from* this
[8] Text: ∧Masters∧
[9] Text: lik∧e∧ness
[10] Text: Scholer *altered to* Scholar
[11] i.e., plagued.
[12] Text: ∧him∧

13 In Letter 6 Wesley expressed his gratitude to Langshaw's brother, William, for the present of a guinea.
14 Text: is [nothing but]
15 Text: ∧ever∧
16 Text: mov[e]ing
17 Text: [more than] ∧truly∧
18 Boyce died on February 7, 1779.
19 Text: whip∧p∧ing
20 *whipping ... Plate.* Langshaw uses a metaphor from horse racing, where riders whipped their horses to urge them on, and a gold or silver plate was awarded to the winner. Langshaw assumes that Worgan and Cooke will compete for the position of Master of the King's Music (or Master of the King's Band), left vacant by Boyce's death. In fact the position was given to John Stanley. See Letter 30, note 9.
21 Johann Christian Bach (1735-82), composer and keyboard performer, was the eighteenth child of Johann Sebastian Bach. Often known as "the English Bach," he spent the latter part of his life in London. Karl Friedrich Abel (1725-87), a player of the viol da gamba and the harpsichord, also settled in England. From 1765 until 1782 J. C. Bach and Abel organized and directed between ten and fifteen concerts a year in London. *DNB; NG*, s.v. "Abel, Carl (Karl) Friedrich," "Bach, Johann Christian," "London, VI. 4(i)."
22 Text: [accompan<y>] ∧go with∧
23 Text: kind [office] ∧ness∧

CHARLES WESLEY TO JOHN LANGSHAW
APRIL 6, 1779[1]

My dear Sir,

Your Son goes on well. He *says* nothing of his own improvement; & I not much. That your Ear must find out. He seldom practices at home less than 5 hours a day. The Afternoon he[2] spends in reading. He is a good deal[3] of his time with us; & never idle. Not one acquaintance has he made in London. My Wife's Sisters, just by, like him as well as we do. Our Concerts, I believe, have been of use to him. Till they were over, I coud not get an hour for answering You.

If I shoud commend Jack's play, You might expect too much. Hear and judge for yourself. I shall only add his Master will lose no credit by him.

It is God, no doubt, who gives us favor in the sight of our Fellow creatures. He is the Giver of every good Gift & Blessing. "In all my ways I acknowledge Thee, & Th<ou>[4] shalt direct my paths."[5]

Charles's Loss is irreparable. But the Doctor[6] told him 2 years ago, "He coud then go on, without Him." He does go on well in a private way, not seeking great things. He has a Set of Organ-Concertos ready for the Press. Dr. Boyce's Music is to be sold next Week by Auction. He did not die rich.

I hope your Partner will have the same comfort in her children as we have in ours.[7] My Eldest Brother was a Father to 19 of us.[8] You may safely trust God for half that number.

Give my love to your Brother, & tell him to call on us whenever he visits London. I hope he has got a Daughter of Abraham.[9] Such he shoud find, or make her.

You need not fear our making Jack a Methodist. I dont wish my own Children to be so called. God, I trust, will make them real Christians that is, Sound Members of the Church of England.[10] Send Jack a word of Advice (which we may second) constantly to attend the Church Service on Sunday -

which almost the whole tribe of Musicians neglect. - Wishing all happiness to you & yours. I remain Your affectionate Servant & Friend

C Wesley

London
    April 6. 1779

—— LETTER NO. 8 NOTES ——

1 Address: Mr Langshaw

2 Text: he[s]

3 Text: ∧deal∧

4 Text: *Script not clear.*

5 See Prov. 3:6.

6 Boyce.

7 Text: *An indecipherable deletion precedes* ours. *Perhaps Wesley was going to write* Charles.

8 See Letter 6, note 5.

9 See Gal. 3:7: "Know ye therefore that they which are of faith, the same are the children of Abraham." See also BCP, Solemnization of Matrimony, final exhortation.

10 Wesley was apprehensive that his brother John's activities might lead to a separation from the Church of England.

9

CHARLES WESLEY TO JOHN LANGSHAW
MAY 17, 1779[1]

London
May 17. 1779

My dear Brother,

"Hands speak for Casca."[2] Hear your Son play, & then tell us how you like him.

Advice is not lost upon him. He goes constantly to church, & labours six days. Let him live up to the doctrines of our own Church, & (as Bishop Beveridge[3] observes) he need not be a better Christian than that will make him.

But the Masters (so called) complain very few *are sound* members of our Church. They aspire to nothing higher. Jack & I will let you have all controversy to Yourself.

My eldest Brother Samuel brought us up, & was a Father to the whole Family.[4]

When young, I had, like Jack, an odd Notion, That one might learn more from old people than from young; which made me covet the company of the former. Jack has no desire for acquaintance of his own age; which is a distinguishing mercy.

Dr. Boyce had revised Charles's Organ Concertos,[5] & given his Imprimatur. His Translation[6] has stopt their being printed. "You & Jack Subscribers?" Two words to that bargain. The first is - Can you afford it? The 2d if you shoud subscribe notwithstanding - Can you dispose of 2 books afterwards? Jack shall play y<ou one>[7] of them - then you will be able to judge.

He talks of visiting you in a month. But his Master (to say nothing of the rest of my family) will not part with him so soon. He must stay here as long as Charles does; which will be 2 or 3 months longer. He is one of our family; & must correspond with us whenever he leaves us. You also will be glad to assure us, he goes on well in the Country. Tis a pleasure to do him any kindness, he takes it so gratefully. Wishing you & y<our>[8] Partner all happiness in your children I remain,

> my dear Sir
> Your faithful friend & Servant
> C Wesley

Jack cannot attain an habit of early rising here, because the family he lives with must not be disturbed by his music. You (I trust) will give him full liberty of conscience. No young man in health requires more than Seven hours sleep. Let him go to bed at Ten & rise at 5. - all the year round. - I had rather leave my Children such an Habit than an Estate - but alas! these mothers -- put in their thwarting oar. Always except Jack's mother & Sam's.

> P.S.
> Partner of the Heavenly Hope
> Travel on & meet me there.[9]

Why else have we met on earth, but that we may spend an happy Eternity together?[10]

LETTER NO. 9 NOTES

[1] Address: Mr Langshaw/ Organist/ Lancaster
Postmark: 18 MA

[2] i.e., actions speak louder than words. In Shakespeare's *Julius Caesar* 3.1, Casca, the first of the conspirators to stab Caesar, says, "Speak, hands for me!"

[3] William Beveridge (1637-1708), Bishop of St. Asaph.

[4] See Letter 6, note 5.

[5] Charles Wesley, Jr.,'s six concertos for organ or harpsichord were published in 1780. See Letter 16.

[6] *Translation* to heaven, i.e., his death.

[7] Text: *The manuscript is damaged.*

[8] Text: *The manuscript is damaged.*

[9] Adapted from Charles Wesley's hymn, "Though absent in body, yet present in spirit," *Hymns and Sacred Poems* (Bristol: Farley, 1742), pt. 2; *Poetical Works*, 2:225:
> Partners of this heavenly hope
> Travel on and meet us there.

[10] Cf. Charles Wesley's "Jesu, we look to thee," *Hymns and Sacred Poems* (1749), 2:322-23; *Collection*, 657; *Poetical Works*, 5:467:
> We meet on earth for thy dear sake,
> That we may meet in heaven.

～ 10 ～

CHARLES WESLEY TO JOHN LANGSHAW
JUNE 2, 1779[1]

My dear Sir,

You have begun counting the days to Jack's Return. We shall be sorry to part with him - was it not to You & his Mother. Most probably she will see him again in August. Your other Son seems a very promising Youth.[2] By & by he may bring his Brother again into favor with Sir John:[3] who, by the way, woud be perfectly reconciled, if he knew exactly how matters stand. Only Charles woud not unnecessarily give offence to Dr. C.[4]

We have not yet thanked you for all your Presents - which proved as good as you wished them.

I lately met with one of your Letters unanswered; but do not always consider Who wrote last. You are almost my only Correspondent. Indeed tis time for me to shake hands with all the world at parting.[5] *Your* night also cometh.[6] Blessed is that Servant whom his Lord shall find watching.[7] May this blessedness be yours & mine. I am

with sincere affection
Your faithful Brother & Servant
C Wesley

London
June[8] 2. 1779

LETTER NO. 10 NOTES

[1] Address: Mr Langshaw/ Lancaster

Erroneously written on the back of the letter in the unknown hand is the date "June 8th 1779".

[2] George Langshaw, who was at school in London. See Letter 11, note 3.

[3] Hawkins.

[4] Cooke.

[5] *shake hands*, in the sense of saying farewell to the world at death. Wesley's mother, Susanna, in writing to her husband on February 6, 1711/12, used the metaphor to describe her refusal to conform to worldly standards: "I have long since shook hands with the world." John Wesley, *Journal*, August 1, 1742.

[6] See John 9:4.

[7] See Luke 12:37.

[8] Text: [M<ay>] June

11

CHARLES WESLEY TO JOHN LANGSHAW
JULY 17, 1779[1]

Dear Sir,

I woud have saved you Postage by making Jack the Bearer of this: but he overpersuads[2] me to send it directly. He talks of leaving us soon. Whenever it is, we shall all miss him.

George I shall try to reconcile to a Servitor's Gown;[3] which several have worn; & afterward Lawn Sleeves.[4]

Charles proposes to publish his Concertos next Winter. Jack will do them justice by his play: & will not appear the last of your country Organists.

Sir John (between friends) overrates his own Musical Abilities. The more Jack excels, the less he will be liked by some - whose judgment is not worth regarding. I *say* nothing of his progress. Hear him yourself,

"& hear[5] with all the malice of a Friend."[6]

Jack will miss our Concert in the winter, if we live so long. Who knows what this Summer may bring forth? The King gives us fair warning:[7] but we have long had reason to fear "This is the Nation to be visited."[8] I doubt whether the Blow will be any more turned aside. We seem to require some national Judgment; for, while his Hand is lifted up *we will not see*.[9]

The Prophet advises well. "Follow after righteousness: it may be ye shall be hid in the day of his fierce anger."[10] God will certainly make a difference betwixt those who fear him & those who fear him not. - Commending You & yours to his Almighty Protection, I remain

dear Sir
Your truly affectionate Servant
C Wesley

London
July 17. 1779

LETTER NO. 11 NOTES

1 Address: Mr Langshaw/ Organist/ Lancaster.
  Postmark: 17 IY

2 Text: overpersuad[ed]∧s∧

3 *Servitors* at Oxford and sizars at Cambridge were students who did menial tasks in college in return for reduced fees. Jack Langshaw's brother George was educated at Charterhouse, the London public school. He was admitted as sizar at Jesus College, Cambridge, in 1782, and never took up residence because of illness. In the school records he is described as the son of "John Langshaw of Westminster," as Langshaw had formerly resided there. When this letter was written, George was at Charterhouse and contemplating entry into Oxford rather than Cambridge. *Alum. Cantab.*; R. C. Arrowsmith, comp., *Charterhouse Register* (London & Chichester: Phillimore & Co, 1974), 228-29.

4 *Lawn sleeves* were part of a bishop's dress. Wesley means that some servitors had become bishops.

5 Text: [& h<ear>]/ "& hear

6 Edward Young, *Love of Fame, the Universal Passion*, 3.9-10:
   Tho' prone to like, yet cautious to commend,
   You read with all the malice of a friend.
For Young's influence on Wesley see Introduction, 5.

7 On June 17, 1779, George III informed Parliament that he had withdrawn his ambassador from Spain in response to the Spanish king's withdrawal of the Spanish ambassador from Britain. George III warned that Britain was in danger of attack from Spain, which was about to enter into an alliance with the American Patriots and France.

8 See Jer. 6:6: "This is the city to be visited."

9 See Isa. 26:11.

10 See Zeph. 2:3: "Seek righteousness, seek meekness: it may be ye shall be hid in the day of the LORD's anger."

12

CHARLES WESLEY TO JOHN LANGSHAW
OCTOBER 26, 1779[1]

Marybone
Oct. 26. 1779

My dear Friend,

    Last Saturday we visited our house in peace, after a long Ramble of 11 Weeks, mostly thro' Wales. Sam[2] at leaving town was threaten'd with a Consumption. Constant Riding has been the appointed means of his Recovery. But we had better not set our heart upon him; since

> All more than common menaces an end,
> A Blaze betokens Brevity of life.[3]

Apply (& let his Mother apply) this doctrine to your promising Jack. Yet I trust he will be spared, to take the whole Family under his Wing.
    He is certainly improved in more things than Music. Charles's First Scholar, Mrs. Luther, a Lady of fashion, & of great discernment told Charles That "Jack was one of the best-bred Youths whom she had seen."[4] Dont tell this to Jack for young fellows, you know, are too apt to be vain. I allow his Father to be a little vain of such a Son.
    Another 6 months Visit woud set him up[5] A.M.[6] Suppose you sent him to Charles next Summer? But Charles is not sure of living till then, therefore had you not better send him to us, *before Winter?*[7] He is capable of much farther Instruction; & Charles will have less & less spare time every Season.
    My one Condition is That he keep early hours. He *must* rise at Six,[8] if he woud attain his point.
    "By straining up the Steep of Excellent."[9] Early rising is good[10] for soul, body, & estate.[11]
    Charles's Concertos are ready for the Press. The Organists say they are much wanted. Jack laughs at difficulties: & will soon be able to teach them Dr.

C. Sir John,¹² or - his Father. Commending you & yours to the Divine Blessing & Protection, I remain,

dear Sir,
Your faithful Friend
& loving Servant
C Wesley.

LETTER NO. 12 NOTES

1. Address: Mr Langshaw/ Organist/ Lancaster
   Postmark: 26 OC
2. Wesley's son, Samuel.
3. Young, *Night Thoughts*, 5.792-93.
4. Mrs. Luther was a regular subscriber to the Wesley concerts. See RAM, Wesley, *passim*.
5. Text: ∧up∧
6. A.M. was the abbreviation for Master of Arts at Oxford and Cambridge. Since Jack Langshaw was not taking a university degree, Wesley is using the letters in an unofficial sense of becoming a "Master" or recognized teacher of music.
7. See 2 Tim. 4:21.
8. Text: Six, [or F<ive>]
9. Young, *Night Thoughts*, 7.704.
10. Text: ∧good∧
11. Cf. BCP, A Collect or Prayer for all Conditions of men: "mind, body, or estate."
12. Cooke and Hawkins.

CHARLES WESLEY TO JOHN LANGSHAW
MAY 11, 1780[1]

> London
> New Chapel, City Road[2]
> May 11. 1780.

My dear Sir,

    I have been long in your debt,[3] but not thro' forgetfulness of you & your Family whom we often talk of, particularly of Jack. His own hands must minister to his necessities, & those of his nearest Relatives. My Eldest Brother was a Father to nineteen of his brothers & sisters.[4]

    We sincerely rejoice with you in the Augmentation of your salary.[5] This also hath God wrought.[6] I hope your Son has learnt of you, to ascribe every Blessing to Him. Tis He who gives us favor in the sight of our Fellow-creatures:[7] and intends every outward Blessing as a Pledge of Spiritual Blessings.[8]

    Charles is hard at work to finish & prepare his Organ Concertos for the Press, against Winter. His Concert hindred their Publication sooner.[9] Your Son will be welcome to his best assistance: & may, if he pleases, get to the Top of his Art. Nature & Industry conquer all things.

    Mrs Langshaw's small, large Family[10] will find her Wheel[11] full employment. Nevertheless my Wife is equally obliged to her.[12]

    We sent our Daughter[13] this morning to Bath in hope to shake off an inveterate Cough, before it ends in a Consumption.

    Does Jack rise as early as his health permits? Let early hours, & Punctuality distinguish him from the whole Tribe of Musicians. Wishing <you & your family Wisdom>[14] & happiness, I remain,

> dear S<ir>[15]
> most sincerely <yo>urs[16]
> C. W<esl>ey[17]

~~— LETTER NO. 13 NOTES —~~

1. Address: Mr Langshaw/ Organist/ Lancaster.
Postmark: 11 MA
2. On November 1, 1778 the City Road Chapel, afterwards known as Wesley's Chapel, was opened.
3. i.e., I have long owed you a letter.
4. See Letter 6, note 5.
5. An increase on Langshaw's £100 per annum. See Letter 1, note 8.
6. Cf. 1 Sam. 11:13; 19:5; 2 Sam. 23:10,12.
7. See Exod. 11:3; 12:36.
8. See Eph. 1:3;
9. See Letters 15 and 16.
10. Text: *An indecipherable character has been deleted.*
11. Spinning wheel.
12. Mrs. Langshaw may have sent a gift to Sarah Wesley.
13. Sarah (Sally) Wesley.
14. Text: *The manuscript is damaged where the seal was broken.*
15. Text: *The manuscript is damaged.*
16. Text: *The manuscript is damaged.*
17. Text: *The manuscript is damaged.*

14

CHARLES WESLEY TO JOHN LANGSHAW
JULY 15 (17), 1780[1]

London
July 17. 1780

My dear Sir,

We rejoice in[2] your Welfare, & your Partner's & family's. Your Brother I shall be very glad to see - that I may remind him of our Master's Word - Beware of Covetousness![3]

Jack's diligence we have no doubt of. It is your fault, if he does not rise early: for what is Precept without example? I had rather leave my Son an habit of early rising, than an Estate.[4]

Jack you shoud send the beginning of January. Charles's Concertos he hopes to publish against the Winter. His Concert begins in January. He woud not dislike a Scholar of yours; for she must know what she is about. Neither can I blame her Mother for scrupling the Entrance.[5] Bach[6] & the first Masters have 6[7] Guineas[8] entrance, &[9] half a guinea a Lesson of 20 minutes. Charles's price is 3 Guineas Entrance, & 3 Guineas a month. He never keeps a Scholar less than an hour: some much longer: for he spares no pains to make his Scholars Musicians. He takes but a few, that he may do them justice, and have time for his own improvement. He has no doubt of having his Number next winter. He has nothing mercenary about him: yet for his own Credit, insists on Entrance. He took it[10] of Miss Carr[11] & taught her the first month gratis; was paid for the next month, & then presented her with 2 years instruction. - His taking a Scholar without entrance woud hinder his taking one with it.

Charles has lost nothing by his Generosity. Some of his Scholars have paid him more than his price. All are satisfied with him. The strictest Master is, I apprehend, the cheapest. Wishing you & yours all happiness in both worlds.
I remain, - dear Sir, - Your faithful friend & Servant

C. Wesley.

LETTER NO. 14 NOTES

1. Address: Mr Langshaw, Organist/ Lancaster
   Postmark: 15 IY
Wesley's date, which is repeated by the unknown hand, is mistaken.
2. Text: [of] ∧in∧
3. Luke 12:15.
4. For early rising, see Letters 9, 12, and 15.
5. *Entrance* was the initial fee for beginning a course of study.
6. Johann Christian Bach. See Letter 7, note 21.
7. Text: 5 *has been altered to* 6
8. For *Guinea* see Letter 4, note 4.
9. Text: ∧&∧
10. Text: ∧it∧
11. *Miss Carr* is listed as a singer and pianist at the Wesley sons' concerts. RAM, Wesley, 33, 72.
    Text: ∧Carr∧

15

CHARLES WESLEY TO JOHN LANGSHAW
SEPTEMBER 25, 1780[1]

Dear Sir,

Yours[2] met me at my return from Bristol. We rejoice to hear of your Family's Welfare: & expect Jack at Christmas, while my Son's Concerts will be rehearsing. His Concertos are in the press. Your Son will soon master them: and in Six months commence Master[3] himself - if he takes time by the forelock: i.e. if he acquires an habit of rising. He must not look to you for an Example, but to us. For most of my life, I have constantly rose at Four, till weighed down by age I am compelld to rest till Five. My children might rise as early as me - but Mamma - Mrs. Lang<s>haw perhaps can make out the sentence.[4] Now I must enter into Articles with my friend Jack. Will he take the trouble to rise at Charles's hour, which is Six, winter & summer?[5] Is it not buying Music too dear? On this *only* condition, my Sons are at his service. He may contract an habit of rising (if his mother & you give leave) before he comes. It is for his good that I lay so much stress upon this. It is good for Soul, body, and Estate.[6] So he will acknowlege, when I am returned to dust[7] -having first left him this invaluable legacy.

My Partner & daughter return thanks for Mrs. L's Present.[8] Perhaps you may find time to visit us with your Son. Was not your Brother *promised* us this year? My best wishes attend your whole Family. Hoping to meet you all in That Day[9] I remain

dear Sir
Your truly affectionate Servant
C. Wesley

London
Sept. 25. 1780.

LETTER NO. 15 NOTES

1 Address: Mr Langshaw,/ Organist/ Lancaster
 Postmark: Only the "2" is visible
Source: The Methodist Collection, Drew University Library.

2 An allusion to a letter from Langshaw that was awaiting Wesley on his return to London.

3 i.e., qualify as Master.

4 i.e., Mrs. Langshaw can complete the sentence. Wesley implies that his wife stands in the way of his insistence on early rising. See also Letter 9.

5 In Letter 9 Wesley advocates five as the hour for rising, but here and in Letter 12 he has become reconciled to six.

6 See Letter 12, note 11.

7 See Gen. 3:19.

8 Mrs. Langshaw's.

9 See Letter 9, notes 9 and 10.

16

CHARLES WESLEY TO JOHN LANGSHAW
DECEMBER 4, 1780[1]

London
Dec. 4. 1780

My dear Sir,

I give Jack credit for behaving well; & for making the best use of his time, on his return to town. Six months close application will quite set him up for A.M.[2]

He knows my single Postulatum,[3] Early & constant Rising. *You* know not the importance of this Habit. I do, & therefore recommend it so earnestly to all my young friends.

You have no right to the Gout, unless you *sit still*. Gentle, but constant, Exercise is the only palliative Cure.

Charles has a Scholar, who in less than a year has learnt all Handel's Lessons, & many of Scarlatti's &c. He comes to my house twice a week, & continues here playing from morning to night.

Another Scholar plays 6 hours every day. In less than 2 years such Players will be perfect in their art.

Send your Answer by Jack. He will find the Concertos finished, & receive your 2 sets. They are printed by Subscription (A Guinea the whole) with all sort of accompaniments.

I shall be glad to see your Brother. My love to him, & to your Partner & Jack. Who brought *us* safe thro' the slippery Paths of youth?[4] He whose grace is sufficient for our Children[5] To his gracious Protection I commend you all, & remain

dear Sir
<Y>ours[6] most affectionately
C. Wesley

LETTER NO. 16 NOTES

[1] Address: Mr Langshaw/ Organist/ Lancaster
Postmark: 4 DE

[2] See Letter 12, note 6.

[3] Text: Postu[mer]latum,

[4] See Joseph Addison's hymn, "When all thy mercies, O my God," *Spectator*, No. 453, August 9, 1712:

> When in the slippery paths of youth
> With heedless steps I ran,
> Thine arm unseen conveyed me safe,
> And led me up to man.

[5] See 2 Cor. 12:9.

[6] Text: *The manuscript is damaged where the seal was broken.*

17

CHARLES WESLEY TO JOHN LANGSHAW
JULY 1, 1781[1]

My dear Sir,

    I had given my Letter to Jack, before your Last came.[2] With great care George may get over the evil which threatens him. Oxford is not a place for "getting money in." If he gets learning without losing his innocence, it is sufficient. He may do, "without calling upon you for help." But then you shoud help him a little, without his calling.[3]

    I have not seen the Magazine.[4] One effect it will have - it will set the Professors[5] upon my Sons to tear them in pieces. Charles's Concertos were advertized more than once or twice. Again I say - Jack may, if he please, make a great Master. We shall rejoice to hear from you. Wishing you & your Partner much happiness in all your children, I remain dear Sir

                              Your faithful friend & Servant
                                          C. Wesley.

Marybone
    July 1.

∽⊖— LETTER NO. 17 NOTES —⊖∾

1 Address: Mr Langhaw (*sic*)
There is no postmark, and the unknown hand on the back reads "July 1st 1781". Wesley dates the letter "July 1" but, as was his frequent habit, makes no reference to the year. Since George Langshaw died on May 23, 1782, and Charles Jr.'s concertos, mentioned here by Wesley, were published late in 1780, this letter must have been written in July 1781.

2 i.e, your last letter. Wesley gave his letter to Jack either to send with other mail to his father or to take with him on his return home. In fact, however, he did not return home until after July 23, the date of another letter that he was to take with him.

3 The evil that threatens George Langshaw must be the illness that proved fatal. George seems to be contemplating the possibility of entering Oxford University. He hopes to be able to live there, presumably as a servitor, without help from his father. See Letter 11, note 3.

4 The *Gentleman's Magazine*, 51 (April 1781): 176-78, reviewed Daines Barrington's *Miscellanies* and briefly alluded to his account of Charles Wesley's sons' attainments as infant prodigies.

5 i.e., professional musicians.

18

CHARLES WESLEY TO JOHN LANGSHAW
JULY 23, 1781?[1]

>   July 23
>   London

My dear Friend,

    I anticipate your joy at the Receipt of this by so welcome a Messenger. We have been in some anxiety both for him & Charles. Their Betters have been pressed to serve their Country:[2] But if the Lord of hosts is with us, we need not fear any Invader.[3] We have received certain intelligence of a Visit within the[4] Fortnight. God can yet deliver us *from* the evil. I rather expect He will deliver us *in* it.[5]

    I must refer you again to Milton - "A grateful mind by owing pays, at once - Indebted & discharged."[6] Jack well deserves more than all the kindness we coud shew him. His mother has the satisfaction of receiving him again - from London - uncorrupted. That *you* may not be disappointed, don't expect too much. I think, he plays so well, that he *may* play as much better as he pleases. But I doubt whether the Country will be his Sphere of Action. My Sons have not seen their last of him. - We shall be glad to hear how he goes on with you. He will make his way - without Sir John's favor. Only let him continue to fear God; & above all things, to seek the kingdom.[7] Commending you all to our Almighty Protector,[8] I remain

>   dear Sir -   Your affectionate Servant
>   C Wesley

──── LETTER NO. 18 NOTES ────

[1] Address: Mr Langshaw
The letter has no postmark, because Jack was its bearer. The writing in the unknown hand gives the date as "July 23d 1781", but the year has been altered from "1780". The letter could not have been written in July 1780, because Jack was in Lancaster (see Letters 13 and 14). 1779 and 1782 are possible years, but Wesley had already written a letter to Langshaw on July 17, 1779, and there is no evidence in the correspondence that Jack visited London in 1782. The most likely year for this letter is 1781.

[2] The Press Gang, which forced men into the army and navy, devoted its attention mainly to the lower classes but sometimes laid hands on people in a higher rank of society.

[3] See Ps. 46:2, 7, 11 (AV, BCP).

[4] Text: [a] ∧the∧

[5] While *deliver us from the evil* clearly alludes to the Lord's Prayer, *deliver us in it* may have in mind BCP, Litany: "In all time of our tribulation ... Good Lord, deliver us."

[6] See Letter 5, note 5.

[7] See Matt. 6:33.

[8] See BCP, Collect for the 4th Sunday after Trinity, "O God, the protector of all that trust in thee...".
Text: Protection *has been altered to* Protector

19

CHARLES WESLEY TO JOHN LANGSHAW
SEPTEMBER 28, 1781[1]

My dear Sir,

Every honest well-informed Subject thinks with the Author of the Poem;[2] which was published to open the eyes of those who are still deluded by the mock-patriots. My Brother's writings have done a great deal towards it.[3] He has abridged all Mr. Galloway's Tracts.[4] Expect 12 of How,[5] & one of the others & the 12 poems, shortly.[6]

I am just returned from Bristol. We shall miss Jack in the winter; but rejoice that you have him safe & sober. He will find the world, the flesh & the devil[7] in every place: therefore he had need pray <m>uch[8] & read the scripture daily. I dont doubt his Progress in Music. It is his business & shoud take up all his working time. He & Charles shoud be constant correspondents. My family salute you & your partner & children. The Lord preserve you all unto That day![9] So prays Your old useless Servant

C. Wesley

London
    Sept. 28. 1781

LETTER NO. 19 NOTES

[1] Address: Mr Langshaw
This letter, which reveals Wesley's views on the American Revolution, was written less than a month before the defeat of the British at Yorktown.

[2] The *Arminian Magazine*, 4 (June 1781): 340, published a poem attacking the American rebels and their British supporters. The poem, though unsigned, may well be the work of Charles Wesley.

[3] John Wesley, *A Calm Address to Our American Colonies* (London: Hawes, 1775); *A Seasonable Address to the more serious part of the Inhabitants of Great Britain* (Bristol: Pine, 1776); *Some Observations on Liberty* (London: Hawes, 1776); *A Calm Address to the Inhabitants of England* (London, 1777).

[4] Joseph Galloway (1730-1803), an American Loyalist, migrated to England in 1778. In a series of tracts about the American Revolution he criticized Britain's conduct of the war and advocated a more aggressive policy. *DNB*. Galloway attended a Wesley concert in 1783. See RAM, Wesley, 16. For his use of the name Fabricius see Letter 20, note 2.

[5] *How* refers to one of John Wesley's extracts from Galloway, either *An Extract of a Letter to the Right Honourable Lord Viscount H--e on his Naval Conduct in the American War* (London: Paramore, 1781) or *An Extract from a Reply to the Observations of Lieut. Gen. Sir William Howe, on a Pamphlet, entitled Letters to a Nobleman* (London: Paramore, 1781). Admiral Viscount (later Earl) Howe was commander of the British North American fleet, and his brother, Lt.-Gen. Sir William Howe, was commander in chief of the American colonies.

[6] Besides the tracts mentioned in the previous note, John Wesley published two other works based on Galloway's writings. They were *An Account of the Conduct of the War in the Middle Colonies. Extracted from a late author* (London, 1780), and *Reflections on the Rise and Progress of the American Rebellion* (London: Paramore, 1780). It is not clear which are the twelve poems that Charles Wesley mentions. His *Hymns for the Nation, in 1782* (London: Paramore, 1781) contain seventeen.

[7] BCP, Collect for the 18th Sunday after Trinity: "...to withstand the temptations of the world, the flesh, and the devil."

[8] Text: *The manuscript is damaged.*

[9] See 1 Thess. 5:23; 2 Tim. 4:18.

CHARLES WESLEY TO JOHN LANGSHAW
DECEMBER 22, 1781[1]

Chesterfield street
Dec. 22. 1781

Dear Sir,

Read Fabricius's most excellent Letters in the Morning Chronicle, this month,[2] & you[3] will see the Cause of all our Misfortunes, & the Remedy. You have some Tracts by the same hand.

If Charles hears farther from[4] Mr. P. or[5] Sir James,[6] he will write to you directly. Meantime he is much obliged to you for your intended kindness.

Your Son George, I hope, as well as Jack, will live to be both a Comfort & an Honor to you. Jack need not fear playing before any Doctor. You dont tell us how he goes on. We hope the best.

You see my thoughts on the present Crisis in the inclosed hymns, written for this day which all my Brother's Societies observe as a Fast.[7]

I have convinced Charles he was a fool to refuse the Scholar you coud have got him, by insisting on Entrance.[8] Tis now, I presume, too late to obtain her. His youth terrifies the mothers from trusting him with their daughters. So many Masters have married their Scholars.

He and Sam are busy, preparing for their Concert.[9] They dont expect[10] to get by it much more than Reputation and increase of Skill. I need not tell you the hearts of the Professors[11] towards them. Yet I dont wish them to make more haste to be rich. What more ought we to wish than Content with food & raiment.[12] The Blessing of God be with you & yours.

Farewell in Christ[13]

LETTER NO. 20 NOTES

[1] Address: Mr Langshaw

[2] Letters under the name Fabricius, a pseudonym of Joseph Galloway, appeared in the *Morning Chronicle* on December 3, 7, and 8, 1781. They criticized the British government for lack of firmness towards British supporters of the rebels and expressed concern about the fate of the American Loyalists. See Letter 19, note 4.

[3] Text: ∧you∧

[4] Text: [about] from

[5] Text: [&] or

[6] The identity of these men is unknown.

[7] John Wesley recorded in his *Journal* for Friday, December 21, 1781, the day before Charles wrote this letter, "We observed all over England as a day of fasting and prayer: and surely God will be intreated for a sinful nation." The catalogue of Charles Wesley's published work does not include anything written specifically for that day. He may be alluding, however, to his *Hymns for the Nation in 1782* (London: Paramore, 1781) or, if they were in manuscript form, his *Hymns for the National Fast, Feb.8, 1782* (London: Paramore, 1782). See Frank Baker, comp., *A Union Catalogue of the Publications of John and Charles Wesley*, 2nd ed. (Stone Mountain, Georgia: George Zimmerman, 1991), 166-67 (nos. 366-68).

[8] See Letter 14, note 5.

[9] The first concert of the brothers' fourth series was on January 31, 1782.

[10] Text: [expl<ore>)] expect (*text of deletion unclear*)

[11] See Letter 17, note 5.

[12] See 1 Tim. 6:8.

[13] This letter has no signature.

CHARLES WESLEY TO JOHN LANGSHAW
JUNE 5, 1782[1]

Dear Sir,

The Flower is cut down[2] - but transplanted to paradise. I thought it cruel, Not to warn you of his danger: but I coud not find in my heart to tell you *all* my fears. - He is at rest: He is safe and happy in the haven.[3] We must wait, till all the waves & storms are gone over us also.[4]

God can make one Son as useful as Two, or as Twenty. He has given my friend Jack a Paternal heart. Be careful for nothing.[5] God will provide for ours, when we are no more seen.

The Influenza stopt my writing sooner. I am slowly recovering from it. All London is in the same Condition.

Poor old Mr. Kelway is at last released: & is, I have reason to hope, in the Quire above. Dr. C. has got his place: but Dr. C. cannot keep it from *his* Successor. What signifies it his grasping at every thing, & carrying every thing, when he must *leave* every thing?[6]

I hope, your Partner has found Him who comforteth the afflicted.[7] She has always David's Comfort "I shall go to Him."[8] I have five children waiting for me in one grave.[9] The days of our mourning will soon be ended.[10] All here join in love with

dear Sir
Your faithful & affectionate
friend
C. Wesley

London
  June 5. 1782

LETTER NO. 21 NOTES

[1] Address: Mr Langshaw.
Wesley sends condolences to Langshaw on the death of his son, George, at the age of 18, on May 23, 1782. See also Letters 10, note 2; 11, note 3; and 17, note 3.

[2] See Job 14:2 and BCP, Burial Service.

[3] Cf. Charles Wesley's "Jesu, lover of my soul." *Hymns and Sacred Poems* (London: Strahan, 1740); *Poetical Works*, 1:259:
> Safe into the haven guide,
> O receive my soul at last!

[4] "Though waves and storms go o'er my head," from "Now I have found the ground wherein." Johann Andreas Rothe, trans. John Wesley, *Hymns and Sacred Poems* (1740), 91-92; *Collection*, 309.

[5] Phil. 4:6.

[6] For Kelway and Cooke (Dr. C.) see Letter 1, notes 14 and 2. Cooke succeeded Kelway as organist at St. Martin-in-the-Fields, and at the same time retained his appointment at Westminster Abbey.

[7] See Ps. 119:50 (AV); 1 Thess. 3:7; BCP, A Collect or Prayer for all Conditions of men, "all those, who are any ways afflicted ... that it may please thee to comfort and relieve them."

[8] See 2 Sam. 12:23.

[9] Of Wesley's eight children five died in infancy: John, Martha Maria, Susanna, Selina, and John James. Only Charles Jr., Samuel, and Sarah grew to adulthood.

[10] See Isa. 60:20.

22

CHARLES WESLEY TO JOHN LANGSHAW
DECEMBER 10, 1782[1]

London
Dec. 10. 1782

My dear Sir,

If "all these things are not added unto us," we should examine ourselves. Do we seek the kingdom *First?*[2] I fear your Brother grew slack, before he grew poor.[3] If he takes care of his soul, God will take care of his body, & of his family also. I write thus in my jealousy of love for him,[4] trusting he will be part of our Crown in that day.[5]

The prospect for the Loyalist brighter, say you? Alas, alas - it is almost a Total Ecclipse![6] They are betrayed deserted, sold into the hands of their Murtherers. Threescore thousand of our Fellow-subjects at New York expect daily to be turned out upon the swords of the Rebels. 2 millions or more will be forced under their Yoke by our infernal Statesmen![7] And shall I not[8] visit for these things, saith the Lord?- If He had not[9] left himself a small Remnant, we had been made long ago as Sodom and Gomorrha.[10]

I dont wonder at your Curiosity for "more particulars." You and your Son have the best right to know them[11] as none woud more rejoice in Charles's success. It is not prudent to commit them to writing. Know in general, Your Conjectures are exactly right. "Where have I been, that I never heard you before? How have they kept you from me?<">[12] &c. &c.- which &c. &c. you must come to have explained.[13]

Charles will not print till he has Subscribers enough to bear him harmless.- His head is not turned by his late success. Perhaps he may be sent for again; perhaps not. "Who wants amusement in the flame of battle?"[14] kindled and kept up by treason and rebellion! My greatest ambition[15] is to pass safely thro' things temporal.[16] Wishing you and Yours the same happiness, I remain,

dear Sir
Your faithful loving Servant
C. Wesley

LETTER NO. 22 NOTES

[1] The letter has no address or postmark on the back.

[2] See Matt. 6:33.

[3] See Prov. 10:4. For William Langshaw see Letter 5, note 11.

[4] See 2 Cor. 11:2.

[5] See 1 Thess. 2:19; 5:4.

[6] After the defeat of the British at Yorktown in October 1781, the victorious Patriots enacted laws against the Loyalists and often confiscated their lands. Many of the Loyalists went to Canada, the Bahamas, or the West Indies. Charles Wesley wrote several poems about them (*The Unpublished Poetry of Charles Wesley*, ed. S. T. Kimbrough, Jr., and Oliver A. Beckerlegge [Nashville: Kingswood Books, Abingdon Press, 1988-92], 1:115-29, 136-40). The British failed in their attempt to secure compensation for the Loyalists and signed preliminary articles of a peace treaty on November 30, 1782. See John Cannon, *The Fox-North Coalition: Crisis of the Constitution, 1782-4* (Cambridge: The University Press, 1969), 33-34.

[7] On March 20, 1782, Lord North resigned as Prime Minister. The Marquess of Rockingham, who supported American independence, was appointed in his place. Rockingham died on July 1, 1782. The Earl of Shelburne succeeded him as Prime Minister and was in office at the time when Wesley wrote this letter. The *infernal Statesmen*, to whom Wesley refers, probably included not only Shelburne, his cabinet, and his negotiator, Richard Oswald, but also Charles James Fox, a strong supporter of American independence. Fox's profligate personal life would further antagonize Wesley. See Cannon, *Fox-North Coalition*, 20-34.

[8] Text: ∧not∧

[9] Text: ∧not∧

[10] See Jer. 5:9,29; 9:9; Isa. 1:9.

[11] Text: ∧them∧

[12] Text: *Editorial insertion.*

[13] Wesley refers to listeners' reactions to Charles Jr.'s performances in the concerts in Chesterfield Street.

[14] Young, *Night Thoughts*, 2.64. Because of preoccupation with the political and military crisis George III may not summon Charles Jr. to perform again at court.

[15] Text: *An additional* is *may be deleted.*

[16] See BCP, Collect for the 4th Sunday after Trinity: "that ... we may so pass through things temporal, that we finally lose not the things eternal."

23
CHARLES WESLEY TO JOHN LANGSHAW
JANUARY 27, 1783[1]

Dear Sir,

We shall always be glad to see Jack. His Master is much pleased with his Music.

Last Thursday we had a blind Organist[2] at our Concert, Scholar who was of the blind Organist of Liverpool. One of Charles's Scholars, Mr Atwood, has made his fortune by his play:[3] & is now sent by the Prince of Wales to Italy.[4]

I dont ask you, or any man, how you like the Peace: for no man knows any thing about it.[5] I hope the Loyal Americans are not Sacrificed.

Wishing you & Yours a length of happy years, I remain

dear Sir
Yours most affectionately
C. Wesley

Chesterfield Street
  Jan. 27. 1783

❧— LETTER NO. 23 NOTES —☙

[1] There is no address, postmark, or date in the unknown hand on the back of the letter, but the word "John" is written there, though not in the same hand as the dates.

[2] Wesley mentions but does not name a blind musician in his list of persons present at the concert on January 23, 1783. RAM, Wesley, 60.

[3] *play*, i.e., playing.

[4] Thomas Attwood (1765-1838) was a composer of both secular and church music. In 1783, when he was a chorister at the Chapel Royal, the Prince of Wales (later George IV) sent him to Italy to study the piano. Three years later he went to Vienna to study under Mozart. He was organist of St. Paul's Cathedral (1796-1838) and the chapel in Brighton Pavilion (1821-38). *DNB; NG;* Shaw, 177-78.

[5] The Treaty of Paris (or Versailles), which concluded the American War, was signed on September 3, 1783, many months after this letter was written. Preliminary articles were signed on November 30, 1782, with the Americans and on January 20, 1783, with France and Spain.

24

CHARLES WESLEY TO JOHN LANGSHAW
NOVEMBER 4, 1783[1]

Dear Sir,

Come when he will, your Son will be welcome to us all. The more pains he takes now in composing, the less he need take, by and by. Three months more with Charles will make him A. M.[2]

I am quite weary of our Concerts, and have a right to spend my last days in peace and quiet. It is not yet settled, whither[3] we shall have a Concert this year or not.[4]

Jack's Fugue is much approved by his Master, who will get credit by him. And I hope your Family will[5] be gainers by your Son's Abilities.

I am entring on my last Stage.[6] Be ye also ready,[7] is our Lord's words to all, as well as to You and your affectionate Servant & Brother

Cha. Wesley.

Marybone
Nov. 4. 1783

LETTER NO. 24 NOTES

[1] Address: Mr Langshaw
[2] See Letter 12, note 6.
[3] i.e., whether.
[4] In fact, concerts were held in 1784, 1785, and 1786.
[5] Text: [w<ill>] your Family will
[6] Text: State *altered to* Stage
[7] See Matt. 24:44; Luke 12:40.

25

CHARLES WESLEY TO JOHN LANGSHAW
MARCH 1784[1]

Dear Sir,

All my Brother's Societies honor the King, because they all fear God.[2] I wish the whole Nation like them in this. The Lovers of his Majesty rejoice in the late Defeat of his Enemies. They threaten again; but the bridle is in their mouth.[3]

We are as happy as You in Jack's prosperity:[4] He will be[5] a Blessing to his Family, and a Credit to his Master. Wishing you truly happy in the love of Christ Jesus I remain

>dear Sir
>Your faithful loving Servant.
>C. Wesley

Written in March 1784

>Who can deny the Patriots their praise?
>All Order is inverted in our days;
>"King, Lords, & Commons" is no more[6] the thing
>But Commons, Lords, & after that- The King:
>We see the Subjects on their Sovereign tread,
>The Crown beneath the Mace, the RUMP above the Head![7]

Marybone

⎯⎯ LETTER NO. 25 NOTES ⎯⎯

[1] Address: Mr Langshaw
The letter has no postmark, and the unknown hand dates it "March 23d 1784". The verse at the end of the letter is dated March 1784.

[2] See 1 Pet. 2:17.

[3] See Ps. 32:9-10 (AV, BCP). This letter provides strong evidence of Wesley's political sympathies. The king's enemies to whom Wesley refers are the political opponents of the Prime Minister, William Pitt, the Younger. When George III appointed Pitt to the office on December 19, 1783, the opposition had a majority in the House of Commons, but by March 1784 it found it difficult to sustain that majority. On March 25 the king announced the dissolution of parliament, which was followed by a general election. When parliament reassembled on May 18, Pitt had a substantial majority. See Cannon, *Fox-North Coalition*, 143-243.

[4] *prosperity*, i.e., success. Jack was already in London during February 1784. He attended the Wesley concert on February 19. RAM, Wesley, 77.

[5] Text: ∧be∧

[6] Text: [not] no more

[7] The verse is in *Unpublished Poetry*, 3:392.

26

CHARLES WESLEY TO JOHN LANGSHAW
MAY 20, 1784[1]

London
May 20. 1784

Dear Sir,

Your Son will be soon forthcoming, and return, we hope[2] a Comfort to you and a Credit to Charles. His future Proficiency will depend on his own diligence, and sobriety.- We shall be glad to see your Brother. My family join in respects to Mrs. Langshaw, & Yourself. Expect from Jack a full and true Account of the Jubilee.[3] I hope the Gout keeps its distance from you. My little strength grows less daily. We must soon expect to leave our children behind us, with

The World before, & Providence their Guide.[4]

I remain, dear Sir, your faithful &
affectionate Servant
C. Wesley.

LETTER NO. 26 NOTES

[1] Address: Mr Langshaw.
The unknown hand erroneously dates it in 1782.

[2] Text: ∧we hope∧

[3] i.e., the Commemoration of Handel, held on May 26, 27, 29, 31, and June 5, 1784. See Christopher Hogwood, *Handel*, Chronological Table by Anthony Hicks (London: Thames and Hudson, 1984), 234-40.

[4] From Milton, *Paradise Lost,* 12.646:
> The world was all before them, where to choose
> Their place of rest, and Providence their guide.

27

CHARLES WESLEY, JR., TO JOHN LANGSHAW, JR. AND CHARLES WESLEY TO JOHN LANGSHAW SEPTEMBER 20, 1784? [1]

> Marybone
> 20th Septr

I thank you my dear Friend for your Letters - I began not to think you had forgot me but that your time was more materially employ'd.

It makes me very happy to hear you give satisfaction. I beleive few Organists in your parts understand the true music better than yourself. I have long been thinking of Publishing again, but am at a loss what it shall be.[2]

A second Grand Concerto I have finish'd - I think it is more in the Geminiani stile than Handel.[3]

Sam's Ode I am certain will please those who are fond of that stile of composition but how few real judges of music are to be found.[4] My two Masters[5] have not left their fellows behind them.

I admire the taste of your good people to use the Italians so: perhaps they are not fond of those kind of voices.[6] Did you ever hear Mara sing? she has wonderful powers.[7]

I find I am not to despair yet of seeing you again in Town.[8]

Remember me kindly to your good Father and beleive me,

> with much esteem
> yours
> C. Wesley.

Dr. Worgan means to bring out some more peices for the Harpsichord. Send me your overture when you have finish'd it.

To Mr Langshaw senr.

Dear Sir,

I can only add a line or two. Jack's Master has been thrown away upon him, if he can be content with being a Player only. He must be a Composer or a Dunce: therefore let him begin to day, & never suffer a day to pass, without composing something.

Remember me to your Brother. He and your whole family, I hope, are well. If I dont see Jack again upon earth, let us meet above.[9] Very few Musicians aspire so high. My Partner salutes you in the true love, hoping to pass an happy Eternity with you.

Yours most faithfully
C. Wesley

⟡— LETTER NO. 27 NOTES —⟡

[1] Address: Mr Langshaw junr.
This letter, the first in this collection by Charles Wesley, Jr., is the first to be addressed to Jack Langshaw. It also contains a note by Charles Wesley to John Langshaw. It has no postmark or date in the unknown hand. Since Charles Wesley died on March 29, 1788, it was written no later than September 20, 1787, and since Kelway, one of the *two Masters* mentioned, died in 1782, it was no earlier than 1782. The allusion to *Sams Ode* (note 4) is consistent with a date in 1784; and since Mara arrived in London for the first time in Spring 1784 and sang at the Handel Commemoration, the letter is not likely to be any earlier than that year.

[2] In 1784 Charles Jr. published eight songs and his Concerto Grosso. *European Magazine*, June 1784, 449; November 1784, 363.

[3] In a postscript to Charles Jr.'s sister Sally, appended to a letter to their mother Sarah Wesley (June 3, 1789), Rebecca Spilsbury alludes to Charles Jr.'s second concerto. MARC, DDWF/26/69.

[4] In a letter to his father on August 22, 1784, Samuel mentioned that he had set Horace, *Odes* 4.4, "Qualem ministrum fulminis alitem," to music for six voices. He had been advised to publish it, and his brother Charles was very pleased with it. MARC, DDWF/15/2 .

[5] Boyce and Kelway. See Letter 1, note 14, and Letter 4, note 5.

[6] The sequence of thought is not clear. Charles Jr. may mean that some individuals or, alternatively, people in general are not fond of Italian-style voices.

[7] Gertrud-Elisabeth Mara (née Schmeling) (1749-1833), a native of Germany, was a leading singer in the Italian style that emphasized purity of tone. NG; Charles Burney, *A General History of Music From the Earliest Ages to the Present Period* (1789) ed. Frank Mercer, 2 vols. (New York: Harcourt Brace and Company, n. d.), 2:893.

⁸ Apparently Jack had told Charles Jr. that he intended to visit London again. It is unlikely that he did so. Sainsbury, *Dictionary*, s.v. Langshaw, John, Jr., says that he visited London three times, and Sainsbury's article may well have been based on information from Charles Jr.

⁹ Cf. Charles Wesley, *Poetical Works*, 2:317-19; *Collection*, 716.
> There shall we meet again
> When all our toils are o'er.

See Letter 9, notes 9 and 10.

SAMUEL WESLEY TO JOHN LANGSHAW, JR.
DECEMBER 26, 1809[1]

Dear Sir

Although you may not have entirely forgotten my Name, yet so long a Time has elapsed since any epistolary Communication between us has occurred, that I should not wonder at the Surprize this hand Writing may for a Moment occasion.-

Therefore altho' John Langshaw & Samuel Wesley have not very lately met either in Person or in black & white,[2] I nevertheless am of Opinion that some Tidings of the *Existence* of each will be acceptable to both.-

The present Occasion of my immediate Application to you, relates to an *Organ*, which it seems is to be constructed for your Quarter of the World, & I understand that several Estimates have been, or are about to be delivered in, from various Makers on the Subject.-

I therefore have taken the Liberty of suggesting to You, that *in my Opinion*, there is no Organ Builder in England whose Work would do him more Credit than *Elliott*,[3] in the present Instance, & should you approve of his Proposals, without being pre=engaged in Favour of some previous Applicant, I do not hesitate to promise that you will not be disappointed in your Choice nor I in Danger of any Disgrace by my Recommendation.-

My own Organ is built by him, & notwithstanding its Limitation to *three* Stops (to which I consented, for the Advantage of an Octave of *double Base*[4] Pedals) the Tone of it is such as to much delight all the Judges who have heard it.

I have not the Pleasure of being known to any of your Family *personally*, excepting your late worthy Father & Brother; but in presenting them my best Respects & Wishes, you will oblige

Dear Sir
Your old (& yet I trust not wholly forgotten)
Friend & Servant
S Wesley

Camden Town.
near London.
    Decr. 26th. 1809

ം⊖— LETTER NO. 28 NOTES —⊖ം

[1] Address: To/ Mr Langshaw/ Organist/ Lancaster.
Postmark: DE 27 1809.
Wesley's son, Samuel, recommends Thomas Elliot as organ-builder at Lancaster, where Jack Langshaw has succeeded his father as organist.

[2] i.e., in writing.

[3] Thomas Elliot (c. 1759-1832), a leading organ-builder, did not build the organ for Lancaster. The task was entrusted to George Pike England. Samuel Wesley had played an Elliot organ at the Royal Institution. Thistlethwaite, 4, 55-57; Boeringer, 1:79; 2:94-95; BL, Eg. MS 2159, Samuel Wesley to Rev. C. J. Smyth, January 10, 1810.
Text: ∧than Elliott, ∧ *in margin*

[4] i.e., Double Bass.

29

CHARLES WESLEY, JR., TO JOHN LANGSHAW, JR.
OCTOBER 17, 1822[1]

My worthy and Dear Friend,

I would not wait for the intelligence of Mr. Gray (who succeeds his Father)[2] to answer your kind Letter; which gave us all pleasure to hear from you at all times and on all Occasions. I am highly pleased with your intended Publication from Corelli, and the elegant, and elaborate Geminiani.[3] His late Majesty Christen'd me, by saying Kelway was *his* musical Son, and I call you *his* Grandson.[4] I met yesterday Dr. Carnaby,[5] who was brought up under Dr. Nares,[6] at the Royal Chapel, who rejoiced to hear that any one, in these degenerate days, would venture such a work, and the Doctor promised me to use all his influence to promote the Publication. I cannot remember what Peices I Perform'd on Gray's Pancras new organ,[7] it was in general selected from Handel, and Corelli, with my humble extempore. - I hear Lincoln[8] has enlarg'd the Organ at Brighton by Command, and that his present Majesty[9] has given the beautiful Chamber Organ, which used to be in the Parlour at Kew Palace, made by Green's Foreman Blyth, to the Chapel on the Green, and Dr. Smith of Richmond, is appointed organist.[10]

I am certain, were it not for the obstinacy, of the noble Directors of the Antient Concert,[11] the old Style would be entirly forgotten, we have a great loss in the Earl of Uxbridge,[12] who was my Friend for near 30 years. You have got my Full Concerto, in Geminiani's manner, which I could not have Perform'd there, because the Author was not *old enough* then, however I had the satisfaction of hearing it well done at Windsor Castle, when his late Majesty honor'd the Author, with his Royal approbation.[13] I think you ought to be well remunerated for the trouble you have taken in the work, and I would advise you to get a good Sum for it. I doubt not all the amateurs of good harmony, and the judicious Professors[14] will give due encouragement. It does you real Credit in every respect, none but a real Master could do it.- I did not make any charge to Birchalls[15] successor for Martini,[16] having had a regard for the Man, I wish'd to promote their Interest, except the persons who go to the Antient the school is not general.[17] They are going to Publish Dr. Green's[18] Anthems by Subscription, but having the 3 volumes of my Master Dr. Boyce, and a large musical Libra<r>y,[19] I do not put my Name to the list. My aged Mother returns her thanks for your kind enquiry, she is now 96. and Sang an Air, on her Birth day last week.[20] My Sister says she[21] cannot alter one word for the better in the Note to your Book.[22] She unites with my Mother and me in kindest Regards to our old Esteem'd Friend, we should rejoice to see you again in Town. I wish we were nearer Neighbours. I very seldom see my Brother but hear he is well.

Would you wish me to inspect the Proof Plates?

>	I am my Dear Friend
>		most faithfully and affectionately
>			Your's,
>				C. Wesley

London
No 14. Nottingham Street
   Marybone.

Oct. 17th 1822.

We have removed here a fortnight ago, and are very comfortable.

When Gray comes to Town, I will get him to write down the Plan and stops of his new organ,[23] the Church is beautiful, though on the whole I give ours the Preference, more Chapels are building in this Parish, the Organists and Organ-Builders are all on the alert, to get the appointments.[24]

LETTER NO. 29 NOTES

1 Address: Mr Langshaw,/ Organist/ Lancaster.
   Postmark: OC 18 1822
   By this time Charles Wesley, Jr., was organist of Marylebone Parish Church. Jack Langshaw had asked Charles Jr. to seek a publisher for music that he had arranged.

2 John Gray (d. 1849), an organ-builder, took charge of the firm on the death of his father, William Gray. He built the St. Marylebone organ in 1818. Boeringer, 1:80,112-14; 2:88-89, 168-69, 323-25; Thistlethwaite, 55.

3 Arcangelo Corelli (1653-1713), Italian composer and violinist. NG. Sainsbury, *Dictionary*, s.v. Langshaw, John, refers to Jack Langshaw's "arrangement of the concertos of Geminiani (Corelli's as they are called) for the pianoforte, violin, and violoncello, which are now in Mr. Wesley's hands, and have met with his and several of his friends' approbation." In his notebook Charles Jr. wrote, "I answered Mr Langshaw at Lancaster" (October 17, 1822), and recorded that on October 18 he took Langshaw's manuscript to the music warehouse. MARC, DDWF/23/16.

4 George III meant that Kelway was the musical son of Geminiani, Kelway's teacher. The king "christened" Charles Jr. in the sense that his statement implied that Charles was the musical son of his teacher Kelway. The reference to *his Grandson* means either that Jack Langshaw was Geminiani's musical grandson because he had learned music with the help of Kelway's lesson book, or that he was Kelway's grandson since Charles Jr. was his teacher.

5 William Carnaby (1772-1839), composer, and organist at Hanover Chapel, Regent Street, London (1823-39). *DNB*.

6 James Nares (1715-83), organist of York Minster (1735-1756) and the Chapel Royal (1756-83). *DNB*; *NG*; Shaw, 12, 320-321.

7 In 1822 John Gray built an organ for the new Parish Church of St. Pancras. Boeringer, 2:325.

8 In 1822 Henry Cephas Lincoln (1789-1864?) built the organ for the Brighton Chapel Royal. Boeringer, 1:117-18; 3:139.

9 George IV (1762-1830) succeeded his father, George III, as king in 1820. He was Prince Regent in 1788-89 and 1811-20 during his father's periods of insanity.

10 The *Chapel on the Green* is St. Anne's Church, Kew. Benjamin Blyth, who worked for Sarah Green after the death of her husband, Samuel Green (1740-96), built the organ for the concert room of Kew Palace in 1801. A *Chamber Organ* was an organ that was privately owned, and this instrument had belonged to George III. Clement *Smith* of Richmond (d. 1826, aged 64) was a Mus. D. of Oxford. Boeringer, 1:77, 80, 94-95; 3:103; *Alum. Oxon.*; *Gentleman's Magazine* 96.2 (1826): 477.

11 The Concerts of Ancient (Antient) Music, held from 1776 until 1848, did not include works written in the previous twenty years. The programmes included many works by Handel, and George III attended frequently. NG, s.v. London VI, 4 (i).

12 Henry Paget, Earl of Uxbridge (d. 1811), father of Wellington's cavalry commander at Waterloo, attended the third Wesley concert in 1781, when he was still known as Lord Paget. RAM, Wesley, 7.

13 The allusion to Geminiani's manner suggests that it is Charles Jr.'s Second Concerto Grosso, written by 1784 (see Letter 27). It was not Charles Jr.'s youth but the recent date of its composition that excluded it from the Ancient Concerts.

14 See Letter 17, note 5.

15 Robert Birchall (c.1760-1819) was a music publisher. After his death the firm was known as Birchall, Lonsdale, & Mills, the successors being Christopher Lonsdale and Richard Mills. *NG*; D. W. Krummel and Stanley Sadie, eds., *Music Printing and Publishing* (New York and London: W. W. Norton & Company, 1990), 175-76, 197. See also Letter 32, note 16.

16 Giovanni Battista Martini (1706-84) of Bologna was a composer, musical scholar, and teacher of composition. *NG*.

17 i.e., except for the audience at the Ancient Concerts, the school represented by Martini is not popular.

18 Maurice Greene (1696-1755), organist at St. Paul's Cathedral from 1718 and the Chapel Royal from 1727, and Master of the King's Music from 1735. *DNB*; *NG*; Shaw, 11, 176-77.

19 Text: *Editorial insertion*.

20 In his notebook for October 12, 1822, Charles Jr. writes: "Read to my Dear Mother, pleasant day, Her Birth Day. An. born 95. The Lord Bless and preserve her. AMEN." MARC, DDWF/23/16.

21 Text: ∧says she∧

22 Perhaps Sally Wesley was commenting on a note that Jack Langshaw had written in his edition of Corelli.

23 The St. Pancras Church organ. See Letter 29, notes 2 and 7.

24 Places of worship that were not the parish church were known as chapels. For organs built for chapels in the parish of St. Marylebone between 1825 and 1830 see Boeringer, 1:90-91, 113; 2:229, 254, 302-03, 314, 337.

30

CHARLES WESLEY, JR., TO JOHN LANGSHAW, JR.
APRIL 3, 1823[1]

London.
Nottingham Street. Marybone (No. 14.)
April 3d 1823.

My Dear Friend,

I begin to think you have not received a Letter I wrote to you, a good while ago, in which I mention'd my having left your Manuscript of Corelli with Messrs. Preston,[2] Dean St. Soho, who said they would immediately write to you, respecting the Publication, the other Shop in the Square declin'd taking it. Mr. Goulding[3] said Antient Authors[4] would not do now.- I suppose the Papers have inform'd you that our rever'd venerable Mother hath departed, at the age of Ninety Six to the Kingdom of Glory.[5] We were in hopes she would have remain'd longer with us, but GOD saw her time was come. Our[6] *irreparable* loss will ever be remembred while we are in this world, and by[7] all who knew her esteem'd and loved her. I hope we shall meet again, where Death, and Mourning are no more.[8] My Dear Sister and I have been through Mercy wonderfully supported. We shall rejoice to see you again in Town. The sight of an old Friend is always cheering and such are you. I have been very little from home except our Church, and the Antient Concert, which I am happy to say is still, well attended by all who love good harmony. The Oratorios (which they call) have been very full I hear, but they could not draw me to such Performances, now Messrs. Smith and Stanley are gone to better Musick.[9] I will thank you to let me know what is your determination, I think it a pity your Corelli, should not be Printed. I beleive I inform'd you Dr. Carnaby, appear'd anxious for the Publication, and said he should be happy to promote the sale. My Sister has been far from well, but thank God is now getting better. We think to take a little trip to Michill Grove Sussex,[10] for a very short time, and in the Autumn if we live mean to go to Bath and <Cli>fton.[11]

My Sister desires to be most kindly remembred to you, Mrs. Langshaw and Family, though we have not yet had the pleasure of being introduced to them. If your good Uncle[12] is living, pray give our kind Respects to him.

> I am My Dear old Friend,
> Most truly
> Your obliged, and faithful
> C. Wesley.

My Brother I hear is well, though we do not often see him.

I have been applied to by the Dean and Chapter of Lincoln to reccomend a new organ for them, I have mention'd Allen, who is an excellent maker.[13] I got an Organ at Bath lik<e>wise[14] for Mr. Gray.[15]

LETTER NO. 30 NOTES

[1] Address: Mr Langshaw./ Lancaster.
Postmark: AP 3 1823

[2] Thomas Preston, publisher, specialized in reprints of earlier editions. Krummel and Sadie, *Music Printing*, 381-82.

[3] George Goulding, music publisher in Soho Square. Krummel and Sadie, *Music Printing*, 267-68.

[4] i.e., old composers.

[5] Sarah Wesley died on December 28, 1822. In his notebook Charles Jr. (MARC, DDWF/23/16) describes her as "very poorly" (December 1, 1822) and "very weak" (December 9, 1822).

[6] Text: our *altered to* Our

[7] Text: ∧by∧

[8] See Rev. 21:4; Isa. 51:11. This sentence echoes some of Charles Wesley's lines. See Letter 9, notes 9 and 10.

[9] After Handel's death John Christopher Smith (1712-95) and John Stanley (1713-86) continued the tradition of writing oratorios. Smith, Handel's assistant and amanuensis, worked with John Langshaw on the Earl of Bute's organ (see Letter 32, note 19). Stanley, who was blind as the result of a childhood accident, was organist at the Temple Church and from 1779 Master of the King's Music. *DNB*; *NG*.

[10] Michel Grove, near Worthing, Sussex, was a manor house that was later demolished.

[11] Text: *Editorial conjecture.*

[12] William Langshaw. See Letter 5, note 11.

[13] This letter assumes that the organ-builder, William Allen, has not yet been given the job at Lincoln Cathedral, but in his notebook for November 5, 1822, Charles Jr. wrote, "Went to Allen. ... I got A. the Lincoln Organ." Allen completed the organ in 1826 (Boeringer, 2:124-26; Thistlethwaite, 49, 52). In letters to the lawyer, Thomas Allan, Charles Jr. later complained that William Allen had not paid him the customary commission for giving his

recommendation (Charles Wesley, Jr., to Thomas Allan, April 19 and May 5, 1828, MARC, DDWes/6/75,76).

14 Text: *Editorial insertion.*

15 Probably the organ of St. Mary's, Bathwick, Bath, built by John Gray in 1820. Thistlethwaite, 47, 554. See Letter 29, note 2.

CHARLES WESLEY, JR., TO JOHN LANGSHAW, JR.
NOVEMBER 24, 1824[1]

London
No. 49. Glocester Place, Portman Square
Nov. 24th 1824.

My Dear Friend,

Yesterday your Friend call'd, when I was out; and this morning brought your Letter by the Twopenny Post.[2] - I am surprized the Instrument did not come from Broadwood,[3] and a new Concerto in Manuscript which I sent you written from the original Score. I hope it is not lost or coppied. I have not vanity to think it will be acceptable to the moderns. Therefore they will not value it. - I inform'd my Brother you and Mr. Heaton subscrib'd to His work and wonder only one copy came. My Sister will send you hers, and when I see Samuel, he shall know your friend hath not got his Copy. I think the Composition Plain, and elegant. Tho' we have long been depriv'd of fine Cathedral Singers, my worthy friend the Rev. Benjamin Mence of St. Pauls,[4] Mr. Clark, & Mr. Pryce of Glocester were eminent in that way, and Bartleman[5] who hath not left any equal to him for voice and judgement. I chose a Piano Forte at Broadwoods lately but I had no idea you had not the one you Commission'd me to get you a long while ago. We have been at the Duke of Norfolk's Castle, Arundel, at Bognor and at Windsor where I went to pay my dutiful Respects to our Gracious King.[6] I only saw Sir W. Knighton,[7] who inform'd me His Majesty is well but His new Organ is not yet finish'd. - Mr. Horn (the German)[8] is now the Organist of St. George's Chapel, but His Majesty only goes to His Private Chapel, Cumberland Lodge. He is making great alterations and improvement at Windsor and the beautiful Park is to have a Grand Monument to the memory of our late Gracious Monarch, whom we all rever'd.-

Do you not intend to take a Trip to Town this Spring? I need not say how glad we both shall be to see you again in this Part of the world.- I have got farther from our Church, but the air is good near the Regent Park,[9] where I can often go and enjoy the fine views. I suppose you know that the Nephew of Richard Worgan is organist of Chester.[10] My acquaintance the late Bishop is translated to Bath and Wells,[11] he is a real admirer of the old Masters.

My Sister joins me in kind Regards to you and your amiable Family.

> I am my Dear old Friend
> most truly your oblig'd
> C. Wesley.

It will allways give me Pleasure to hear from you; I regret I have not a Frank.[12] -

A Lady showed me at Windsor a Manuscript Book which belong'd to the late organist Dr. Aylward[13] of Mr. Kelways, but on perusing it, I perceiv'd it to be nearly the same with the Printed Lessons, which were too hard for general Performers. I remember Dr. Boyce said I never heard them, till you Perform'd them. They are I think much like Geminiani, and Masterly Composition, but very hard.

LETTER NO. 31 NOTES

[1] Address: Mr Langshaw/ Lancaster.
Postmark: NO 24 1824

[2] Jack Langshaw's friend presumably mailed the letter to Charles Jr., when he could not deliver it in person. The *Twopenny Post* was the London District Post. Howard Robinson, *The British Post Office: A History* (Princeton: Princeton University Press, 1948), 196-98.

[3] Broadwood was the name of the leading piano-making firm in England. Its founder was John Broadwood (1732-1812). NG.

[4] Benjamin Mence (c.1722-1796), minor canon of St.Paul's Cathedral (1750-67), Vicar of St. Pancras (1750-96), and Rector of All Hallows, London Wall (1758-96), was a leading counter-tenor who was on good terms with the Wesley family. *Alum. Cantab.*; *Gentleman's Magazine* 66.2 (1796): 1116; Charles Wesley, Jr., Anecdote, n.d., Woodruff.

[5] James Bartleman (1769-1821), a bass singer, was trained under Benjamin Cooke, became a chorister at Westminster Abbey, and was befriended by Sir John Hawkins. *DNB*.

[6] Charles Jr. hoped that George IV would obtain a better appointment for him and wrote to the king and other members of the royal family, asking for their help. He was unsuccessful.

[7] Sir William Knighton (1776-1836) was George IV's adviser.

⁸ Karl (Carl) Friedrich Horn (1762-1830) was organist at St. George's Chapel, Windsor (1824-30). Horn and Samuel Wesley issued an edition of Bach's *Organ Trios* (1809-10) and *Well-tempered Clavier* (1810-13). *DNB*; *NG*; Shaw, 348.

9 Portman Square, from which this letter was written, is nearer to Hyde Park than to Regents Park. The Dorset Square house, in which the Wesleys resided in 1825, was near to Regents Park.

10 *Richard Worgan* was the son of John Worgan. Thomas Haylett was organist of Chester Cathedral from 1824 until 1840. *NG*, s.v. "Worgan, John"; Shaw, 69.

11 George Henry Law (1761-1845), Bishop of Chester (1812-24) and Bishop of Bath and Wells (1824-45). *DNB*. Charles Jr.'s notebooks provide evidence of his meetings with Law (e.g., May 17, 1822, MARC, DDWF/23/16).

12 Members of parliament and other government officers received franking privileges, enabling letters that bore their signature to be mailed free of charge. These officers often gave franked sheets to others, to enable them to avoid postal fees.

13 Theodore Aylward (c.1730-1801), organist from 1788 of St. George's Chapel, Windsor. *DNB*; *NG*; Shaw, 347.

CHARLES WESLEY, JR., TO JOHN LANGSHAW, JR. NOVEMBER 1, 1825.[1]

> London,
> No. 1. New Street[2] Dorset Square,
> near North Baker Street, Regent Park.
> Nov.1. 1825.-

My Dear Friend,

Mr. Mason last Sunday brought me your Letter.[3] My Sister and I have been in Wales, and lately return'd from Buckland House, the Antient Mansion of Mr. Thynne Howe Gwynne our late Mother's near relation, where we were received with old Friendly hospitality.[4] - The Country is beautiful, but we could not get any Harp Performer. They are I hear only to be met with *now* in North Wales. Sir W. W. Wynne[5] hath a fine Performer at his Seat. When I came to Bristol the Dean and Chapter requested me to Perform at the Cathedral, for the annual meeting of the Sons of the Clergy; and I hear they had a larger collection than usual.- I likewise Perform'd on an organ at an other Church where Mr. Handel used to go, when on a visit to the Rector the Revd. Mr. Broughton, an intimate Friend of his,[6] and He Compos'd Part of the Messiah at the Rectory.[7]- I have thought of what you remark'd in Handel's Lessons, on perusing Purcell's Orpheus Britanicus I see he hath often put ♯ for ♮ and ♭. &c- we are in this day more easy to mark the proper Sharps & flats &c- My Brother will take Dr Crotch's Station[8] this year to Lecture at the Royal Institution in Albermarle St. The Doctor says he is tired of the place. - Samuel likewise takes the Organ at Covent Garden the ensuing Lent. - I do not mean my Oratorio to go before the Public. Lord Darnley[9] kindly offer'd me the use of Hanover Square Room,[10] where the Antient Concert is, but hearing I was to remunerate the Band, I declin'd accepting his Lordship's offer.-

We have a select Set of good Performers at a private house, many good Amateurs, and Professors, where I can hear the effect without expence.

Your Voluntary is admirable, and the modulation, I think masterly. You have not studied the old Masters in vain. I think you would do well, to Publish it, not being too hard for the generality of Players. Mr. Mather an admirable organist is charm'd with it.[11]-

If you should take a trip to Town this next Spring, I hope you will hear Elijah.[12] -

I have Compos'd Mason's Caractacus,[13] and Many Anthems, and the dedication of the Temple which I have only heard by myself on my old organ.

My Sister desires her kind remembrance to you and Mrs Langshaw in which I join and am

My Dear Friend
Your's most truly
C. Wesley.

When leisure and opportunity will allow, I shall be glad to hear from you, and particularly that you are coming to London.-

Our new Rector does not chuse any Voluntaries, therefore we only have Psalm Tunes, with an interlude extempore.[14] The People Complain of it, being partial to your old Friend - your Anecdote of the Bates Family amused me. He was a good Conductor, but no great Performer.[15]

I would have sent you the Set of Lord Fitzwilliam's Scarlat<t>i but Burchall[16] says, he has destroy'd the Plates, because they had not a general sale, which I regret.-

I had great trouble in selecting them. All His curious musical library, is left to Kings College Cambridge. My Brother & Hawes[17] mean to publish them by subscriptions.

I suppose you know His late Majesty gave Lord Butes organ <to>[18] which Smith and your Father put the barrels to the late Earl of Uxbridge.[19]

⟡— LETTER NO. 32 NOTES —⟡

[1] Address: John Langshaw, Esqre/ Lancaster./ fowd by /T. Mason Esqre.
[2] Text: ∧New Street∧
[3] Presumably Mason had been collecting Charles Jr.'s correspondence during his absence . He is not to be confused with Mason, the poet, mentioned later in this letter.
[4] Gwynne's daughter had received music lessons from Charles Jr. Thynne H. Gwynne, to Charles Wesley, Jr., March 20, 1793, MARC, DDWF/22/27.

5 Sir Watkin Williams-Wynn (1773-1840), fifth baronet, was member of parliament for Denbigh and Lord Lieutenant of the county.

6 Thomas Broughton (1704-74) provided the libretto, based on Sophocles's *Women of Trachis*, for Handel's *Hercules* in 1745. When he became Vicar of Bedminster, Broughton moved to Bristol. *DNB*.

7 Charles Jr. seems to have confused Handel's *Messiah* with another of his oratorios, *Jephtha*. Handel remained in London while he was composing *Messiah* in 1741. In 1751, however, between composing the second and third acts of *Jephtha*, Handel visited Bath and Cheltenham to take the waters for his failing eyesight. At that time he also visited Bristol. Newman Flower, *George Frideric Handel*, rev. ed. (London: Granada, 1972), 272-73, 321; Hogwood, *Handel*, 287, 291.

8 William Crotch (1775-1847), composer and organist, was the first principal of the Royal Academy of Music. *DNB*; *NG*; Shaw, 213.

9 John Bligh, fourth Earl of Darnley (1767-1831).

10 Hanover Square Rooms, which were opened in 1775, were the site of many important concerts. J. C. Bach, Abel, Haydn, Liszt, Clara Schumann, and many other famous musicians appeared there. *NG*, s. v. London, VI. 5 (ii).

11 In 1826 Charles Jr. invited Mather to officiate on the St. Marylebone Church organ (Charles Wesley, Jr., to Mr. Mather, October 30, 1826, Woodruff).

12 An oratorio written by Charles Wesley, Jr.

13 William Mason (1724-97), an Anglican clergyman, was a poet and dramatist. Charles Jr. composed music for his play *Caractacus*. *DNB*.

14 Voluntaries were normally played at the beginning and end of the service and after the first lesson or before the sermon. The new rector, John Hume Spry, was appointed on August 3, 1825. George Hennessy, *Novum Repertorium Ecclesiasticum Parochiale Londiniense* (London: Swan Sonneschein & Co., 1898), 323.

15 Joah Bates (1740-99) conducted the Concerts of Antient Music. In 1798 he selected another candidate, John Immyns, in preference to Samuel Wesley as organist of the Foundling Hospital. *NG*; Lightwood, *Samuel Wesley*, 92-94.

16 i.e., Birchall. See Letter 29, note 15. Since Birchall was dead, Charles Jr. is referring to the firm rather than to an individual.

17 William Hawes (1785-1846) was a man of many parts. He was master of the choristers at St. Paul's Cathedral and the Chapel Royal, director of opera at the Lyceum Theatre, London, a composer, conductor, organist, and music publisher. *DNB*; *NG*.

18 Text: *Editorial insertion*.

19 The Earl of Bute's organ was built during the 1760s for his residence at Luton Park. It could be used either as a barrel organ or as an organ to be played with the fingers. Barrel organs were played by turning a handle, and the music was set on removable barrels with metal pins. John Christopher Smith, Handel's amanuensis, adapted the music for Bute's organ, and Langshaw fixed the pins to the barrels. This organ was destroyed in a fire in 1843, but most of the barrels had already been transferred to another instrument, made by Alexander Cumming for Bute's residence at High Cliff, near Christchurch, Hampshire. Cumming records that after Bute's death the organ was bought by the Earl of Shaftesbury, whose son sold it to Cumming in 1812. Charles Jr.'s statement that George III gave it to Uxbridge, who died in 1811, is inconsistent with Cumming's account. *NG*, s.v. Barrel Organ; Boston and Langwill, *Barrel-Organs*, 62; Ord-Hume, *Barrel Organ*, 88-94, 462.

33

CHARLES WESLEY, JR., TO JOHN LANGSHAW, JR.
JANUARY 11, 1827[1]

My Dear old Friend,

    I have thought it a long time since I have heard from you, but your Son[2] kindly call'd on us, which gave us real Pleasure, though I regret at that instant I was going out. He Promised to meet me at the Church, but he did not, I wanted to appoint another time that we might have more of his Company.

    I am glad he has chosen the Clerical Profession, and doubt not he will be a worthy member of the Church of England. We have been Westward this Summer, but my Sister has had an Erisipolis,[3] and her Eyes are very weak, she is not able to read or write, but the Physicians say it is not in the Eyes but the System. We are much mortified, respecting your amiable Son, fearing he hath taken umbrage and I have lost his address. When he again comes to Town I hope we shall have the pleasure of his Company. He inform'd me you have heard of my Brothers Publication from Lord Fitzwilliam's Library at Cambridge, the words Handel Set from my Father's Poems are charming in the true Church German style.[4] Mrs. Rich no doubt presented them to Handel, you know when he left the Opera House.[5] Mr. Rich the manager of Covent Garden Theatre offer'd his house, where the great musician Perform'd his later Operas, and Oratorios during the Lent Season. My Brother is engag'd to Lecture at the Royal Institution this Season,[6] and at the Leicester Institution therefore will have full imployment. I have had my Oratorio of Elijah Perform'd in a Private way, though Lord Darnley[7] offer'd me the Concert Room, but I would not venture to Pay the large band, it requir'd, nor would it have been prudent, for the last and only Public Concert we had at the old Antient Music Room did not answer, because we neglected to engage the Late Mrs. Billington, who was just arived in England.[8] Do you never intend to come to Town again? We shall be truly glad to see you again.- My Sister joins in kind Regards to you Mrs. Langshaw and Family.

> I am Dear Mr. Langshaw
> your affectionate and obliged
> old Friend
> C Wesley

Our Church has undergone an alteration and young Grey[9] has wonderfully improved our organ, by filling up the Pipes which was done by Lord Kenyon[10] having West's Picture taken away.[11]

> London.
> No. 1. New Street, Dorset Square
> near
> North Baker Street.

Jany 11th 1827.

I hear Sir G. Smart[12] is coming from Bath to conduct what they call Oratorios, how different to my old Friend Mr. Stanley,[13] I only go to the Antient Concert, and chiefly of a Morning, for we keep early hours.

Let me hear from you when opportunity of Leisure will allow.

There is at Cambridge, a good deal of Handel's own writing which only Mr. Smith[14] could make out, and fine Choruses of Columba whom Dr. Boyce approv'd[15] and much vocal music by Paradies whose Lessons of course you know.[16]

— LETTER NO. 33 NOTES —

[1] Address: Mr Langshaw./ Lancaster.

[2] Jack Langshaw's son, George (1806-48), was educated at Lancaster and Sedbergh schools and St. John's College, Cambridge. He was Rector of St. Andrew's, Cambridge, from 1835 until his death. *Alum. Cantab.*

[3] i.e., erysipelas.

[4] In 1826 Samuel Wesley discovered three hymn-tunes by Handel in Fitzwilliam's Library, Cambridge, set to words by Charles Wesley. He published them in the same year. The first, known as "Cannons," was set to "The Invitation" ("Sinners, obey the Gospel word"), the second, known as "Fitzwilliam," to "Desiring to Love" ("O, Love divine, how sweet thou art"), and the third, known as "Gopsal," to "On the Resurrection" ("Rejoice, the Lord is King!"). Samuel Wesley, *Wesleyan-Methodist Magazine* 49 (1826): 817; Lightwood, *Samuel Wesley*, 193-99.

[5] John Rich (c. 1682-1761), a theatrical manager and pantomimist, built the Covent Garden Theatre, which he opened in 1732. His second wife, an actress, gave up the stage after her conversion to Methodism. *DNB; NG.* Handel, a friend of the Riches, leased Covent Garden Theatre for various performances, and Sarah (Sally) Wesley, in a letter to

the Rev. John Gaulter, October 25, 1826, indicates that the connection with Mrs. Rich led Handel to write the tunes. *Wesleyan-Methodist Magazine* 49 (1826): 817.

6 The Royal Institution was founded in 1799 for scientific research.

7 See Letter 32, note 9.

8 Elizabeth Billington (1768-1818) was one of the most famous English singers of her day. *DNB*; *NG*.

9 Gray (spelt Grey here) was responsible for building the St. Marylebone organ. See Letter 29, notes 2 and 7.

10 George Kenyon, second Baron Kenyon (1776-1855).

11 Benjamin West (1738-1820), the American painter, did most of his work in England. Two of his paintings, "The Nativity," and "The Angels appearing to the Shepherds," were above the altar in St. Marylebone Church. When Gray renovated the organ in 1826, the larger of the paintings, "The Angels," was removed. Helmut von Erffa and Allen Staley, *The Paintings of Benjamin West* (New Haven and London: Yale University Press, 1986), 326-31 (nos. 301, 307).

12 Sir George Thomas Smart (1776-1867), an organist of the Chapel Royal, was the leading English conductor of his day. *DNB*; *NG*; Shaw, 15-16.

13 For Stanley and Oratorios see Letter 30, note 9.

14 John Christopher Smith. See on Letters 30, note 9, and 32, note 19.

15 Giovanni Paolo Colonna (c.1637-1695) was an Italian composer and organist. *NG*. According to Burney, *General History of Music*, 2: 537, "It was the opinion of the late Dr. Boyce, that Colonna was Handel's model for choruses accompanied with many instrumental parts, different from the vocal." The Latin equivalent of Colonna is Columna, not Columba.

16 Pietro Domenico Paradies (or Paradisi) (1707-1791) was an Italian composer who for several years resided in London. *NG*.

INDEX OF NAMES

Abel, Karl Friedrich, 30, 31, 85
Addison, Joseph, 5, 49
Allan, Thomas, 78, 79
Allen, William, 7, 78
Arrowsmith, R. C., 39
Attwood, Thomas, 7, 62, 63
Aylward, Theodore, 81, 82

Bach, Johann Christian, 30, 31, 44, 45, 85
Bach, Johann Sebastian, 8, 31
Baker, Frank, xiii, 13, 57
Barrington, Daines, 4, 51
Bartleman, James, 7, 80, 81
Bates, Joah, 84, 85
Beckerlegge, Oliver A., xiii, 13, 61
Beveridge, William, 34, 35
Billington, Elizabeth, 7, 86, 88
Birchall, Robert, 7, 74, 76, 84, 85
Blyth, Benjamin, 7, 73, 75
Boeringer, James, xv, 12, 13, 72, 75, 76, 78
Boston, Noel, 12, 85
Boswell, James, 20
Boyce, William, 6, 7, 8, 23, 24, 30, 31, 32, 33, 34, 68, 69, 74, 81, 87, 88
Bridgeman, George T. O., 12
Broadwood, John, 80, 81
Broughton, Thomas, 83, 85
Burney, Charles, 69, 88
Bute, Earl of, 1, 78, 84, 85

Cannon, John, 61, 66
Carnaby, William, 73, 75, 77

Carr, Miss, 44, 45
Charlotte, Princess, 7
Coke, Thomas, 4, 13
Colonna, Giovanni Pietro, 88
Cooke, Benjamin, 1, 2, 6, 17, 18, 19, 20, 21, 22, 24, 28, 30, 31, 36, 37, 40-41, 58, 59, 81
Corelli, Arcangelo, 4, 17, 22, 73, 75, 76, 77
Cowper, William, 4
Crotch, William, 83, 85, 86
Cumming, Alexander, 85

Darnley, Earl of, 83, 85, 86

Edwards, F. G., 13
Elliot, Thomas, 8, 71, 72
England, George Pike, 13, 72
Erffa, Helmut von, 88

Fabricius, see Galloway, Joseph
Fétis, F. J., 12
Finzi, Gerald, 13
Fletcher, John, 3, 12, 23
Flower, Newman, 85
Fox, Charles James, 61

Galloway, Joseph, 5, 54, 55, 56, 57
Garrick, David, 3
Gaulter, John, 88
Geminiani, Francesco, 4, 7, 8, 18, 21, 22, 68, 73, 75, 81

George III, 6, 7, 38, 39, 65, 66, 73, 75, 80, 84
George IV, 7, 62, 63, 73, 75, 80, 81, 87, 88
Goulding, George, 77, 78
Gray, John, 7, 8, 73, 74, 75, 78, 79, 87, 88
Gray, William, 73, 75
Green, Samuel, 18, 73, 75, 83, 87, 88
Green, Sarah, 75
Greene, Maurice, 74, 76
Gwynne, Thynne Howe, 83, 84

Handel, George Frideric, 4, 7, 8, 17, 21, 29, 48, 67, 68, 69, 73, 75, 78, 83, 85, 86, 87-88
Hawes, William, 84, 85
Hawkins, Sir John, 19, 20, 27, 28, 36, 37, 38, 41, 52, 81
Haydn, Franz Joseph, 8, 85
Haylett, Thomas, 82
Hennessy, George, 85
Hildebrandt, Franz, 13
Hogwood, Christopher, 67, 85
Horace, 69
Horn, Karl Friedrich, 8, 80, 82
Howe, Adm. Viscount (later Earl), 54, 55
Howe, Lt.-Gen. Sir William, 54, 55

Jackson, Thomas, 13
Johnson, Samuel, 3, 20

Kelway, Joseph, 6, 7, 17, 18, 21, 22, 58, 59, 69, 73, 75, 81
Kenyon, Lord, 87, 88
Kimbrough, S. T. Jr., xiii, 61
Knighton, Sir William, 80, 81
Krummel, D. W., 76, 78

Langshaw, George (son of John), 1-2, 5, 18, 36, 37, 38, 39, 50, 51, 56, 58, 59
Langshaw, George (son of John Jr.), 86, 87
Langshaw, James Pearson, 2
Langshaw, John,
  career, 1-2, 12
  comments on music and musicians, 17-18, 29, 30
  his family, 1-2, 17, 18, 21, 27, 42, 46, 50, 54, 69
  organ mechanic, 1, 12, 78, 84, 85
  salary, 17, 42

Langshaw, John, Jr. (Jack),
  composer and editor, 2, 12, 64, 69, 73, 77, 84
  early rising, 6, 21, 23, 35, 40, 42, 44, 46, 48
  his family, 78, 86, 87
  organist, 2
  pupil of Charles Wesley, Jr., 1, 2, 17-39, 48-53, 65-67
  pupil of Cooke, 1, 2, 17-20
Langshaw, Mary (wife of John), 21, 27, 35, 36, 40, 42, 43, 46, 47, 50, 54, 58, 67, 78
Langshaw, William (brother of John), 25, 26, 27, 28, 29, 31, 32, 44, 48, 60, 61, 67, 69
Langwill, Lyndesay G., 12, 85
Law, George Henry, 81, 82
Lightwood, James T., 13, 85, 87
Lincoln, Henry Cephas, 7, 73, 75
Liszt, Franz, 85
Lonsdale, Christopher, 76
Luther, Mrs., 40, 41

Mara, Gertrud-Elisabeth (née Schmeling), 7, 68, 69
Martin, Charlotte Louisa, 9
Martini, Giovanni Battista, 74, 76
Mason, Mr., 83, 84
Mason, William, 8, 84, 85
Mather, Mr., 84, 85
Mence, Benjamin, 80, 81
Mills, Richard, 76
Milton, John, 5, 26, 52, 67
Mornington, Earl of, 4
Mozart, Wolfgang Amadeus, 8, 63

Nares, James, 73, 75
North, Lord, 61

Oglethorpe, James, 4
Ord-Hume, Arthur W. J. G., 12, 85
Oswald, Richard, 61

Paradies (or Paradisi), Pietro Domenico, 87, 88
Peel, (later Sir) Robert, 2, 12
Pitt, William, the Younger, 6, 66
Preston, Thomas, 7, 77, 78
Prince of Wales, see George IV
Prince Regent, see George IV

Purcell, Henry, 4, 83
Rich, John, 86, 87
Rich, Mrs., 86, 87-88
Robinson, Howard, 81
Rockingham, Marquess of, 61
Roper, William Oliver, 12
Rothe, Johannes Andreas, 59

Sadie, Stanley, xvi, 76, 78
Sainsbury, John S., 12, 70, 75
Scarlatti, Domenico, 7, 8, 17, 21, 22, 29, 30, 48, 84
Schumann, Clara, 85
Shakespeare, William, 5, 35
Shaftesbury, Earl of, 85
Shaw, Watkins, xvi, 18, 24, 63, 75, 76, 82, 85, 88
Shelburne, Earl of, 61
Smart, Sir George Thomas, 87, 88
Smith, Clement, 73, 75
Smith, John Christopher, 77, 78, 84, 85, 87, 88
Smyth, C. J., 72
Sophocles, 85
Spilsbury, Rebecca, 69
Spry, John Hume, 85
Staley, Allen, 88
Stanley, (Charles) John, 31, 77, 78, 87, 88
Suter, Sarah, 9

Thistlethwaite, Nicholas, xvi, 72, 75, 78, 79
True, W. J., 12

Uxbridge, Earl of, 73, 75, 84, 85

Wellington, Duke of, 4, 75
Wesley, Charles,
  and the American Revolution, 5-6, 38, 39, 54, 55, 56, 57, 60-63
  and the Church of England, 32, 33, 34
  and English literature, 5, 25, 26, 35, 39, 41, 49, 52, 61, 67,
  his family, 1, 3-5, 42, 58, 59
  interest in music, 3-6
  early rising, 6, 21, 23, 35, 40, 42, 44, 46, 48
  and Methodism, 6, 32, 33, 65
  his sons' concerts, see Wesley, Charles, Jr.
  sympathy for George III and Pitt the Younger, 6, 65, 66
Wesley, Charles, Jr.,
  composer, 4, 8, 32, 34, 38, 40, 42, 44, 46, 48, 50, 51, 61, 68, 73, 75, 80, 83, 84, 86
  concerts with his brother, 3-5, 27, 28, 30, 32, 38, 40, 44, 46, 56, 60, 61, 62, 64, 66
  infant prodigy, 6
  later career, 6-8
  organist, 7, 24, 73, 83
  and the Press Gang, 52
  pupil of Boyce, 30, 32
  and royal family, 6, 73, 80
  teacher, 1, 27, 29, 40, 44, 48, 56, 62,
Wesley, Eliza (granddaughter of Charles), 13
Wesley, John, 4, 37, 54, 55, 56, 57, 65
Wesley, Samuel (father of John and Charles), 27, 28
Wesley, Samuel, Jr. (brother of John and Charles), 27, 28, 32, 34, 42
Wesley, Samuel (son of Charles), 1, 3, 7, 8, 9, 12, 13, 17, 28, 35, 50, 51, 52, 56, 68, 69, 71, 72, 80, 82, 83, 84, 85, 86, 87-88
Wesley, Samuel Sebastian (grandson of Charles), 3, 9
Wesley, Sarah (née Gwynne, wife of Charles), 3, 7, 17, 18, 21, 27, 35, 46, 47, 69, 74, 76, 77, 78
Wesley, Sarah (Sally, daughter of Charles), 7, 17, 18, 42, 43, 69, 74, 76, 77, 80, 83, 84, 86, 87
Wesley, Susanna (mother of John and Charles), 37
West, Benjamin, 8, 87, 88
Williams-Wynn, Sir Watkin, 83, 85
Worgan, John, 23, 24, 29, 30, 31, 68, 82
Worgan, Richard, 81, 82
Young, Edward, 5, 38, 39, 40, 41, 60, 61

and I hear they had a la[rge]
I likewise Perform'd on a[n]
when Mr Handel used to [play]
Rector the Revd Mr B[rooks?]
of his, and He Compos'[d]
at the Rectory — I have
in Handel's Lessons, on [which]
Lantous I see he hath ofte[n]
we are in this day more
Sharps & Nats re— My B[rother]
takes this year to [lecture]
in Albemarle St. Mr D[r]
Samuel likewise takes the
the ensuing Lent — I
go before the Public. Lord [?]
The use of Hanover Sqr R[ooms]
Concert is, but having I [?]